What prophet was [barcode: S0-ARO-722] **angel?** *(See page 25)*

Where is Satan's final resting place? *(See page 13)*

What apostle was released from prison by an angel? *(See page 23)*

What was the Unrighteous Bible? *(See page 175)*

What scholar, riding on horseback, divided the New Testament into verses? *(See page 173)*

Who had a vision of the Lord on a sapphire throne? *(See page 33)*

Who had seven sons that were attacked by an evil spirit? *(See page 15)*

What book of the Bible mentions a talking altar? *(See page 63)*

Who produced the first printed Bible? *(See page 209)*

What was the Standing Fishes Bible? *(See page 175)*

. . . and more than 1,500 other challenging questions about angels, demons, miracles, visions, and how the Bible came to be written and translated.

The Best of
Bible Trivia
◇ 3 ◇

ANGELS
DEMONS
SCROLLS &
SCRIBES

J. STEPHEN LANG

LIVING BOOKS®
Tyndale House Publishers, Inc.
Wheaton, Illinois

Front cover illustrations:
King, Scroll, and Angel copyright © by Ron Wheeler;
Locust copyright © by Michael Hackett; City on Fire
copyright © 1989 by Joseph Miralles

*The Best of Bible Trivia 3: Angels, Demons, Scrolls
and Scribes* is selections from *The Complete Book of
Bible Trivia,* copyright © 1988 by J. Stephen Lang,
published by Tyndale House Publishers, Inc.

Scripture quotations, unless otherwise noted, are
from the King James Version of the Bible.

Living Books is a registered trademark of Tyndale
House Publishers, Inc.

Library of Congress Catalog Card Number 89-51308
ISBN 0-8423-0466-5
Copyright © 1988 by J. Stephen Lang
All rights reserved
Printed in the United States of America

96 95 94 93 92 91
9 8 7 6 5 4 3 2 1

To Mark Fackler,
who is a friend of the Bible
and who understands laughter

Contents

Part 5: Quote, Unquote

Part 6: Books, Authors, Translators

Part 7: . . . And Things Left Over

Preface

Can we speak of *the Bible* and *trivia* in the same
breath? Can this inspired document that is pored over
with great seriousness by pastors, scholars, and lay
people provide material for leisure—or even laughter?

It can. As I began writing these trivia books, I became
convinced that the Bible, the divine book through which
God's Truth shines, is also an earthy, human collection of
people and incidents that cannot help but amuse (as well as
enlighten) a reader. I believe that the Bible has come down
to us through God's initiative. I also believe that God chose
to present his truth through stories, oracles, and letters that
not only inspire us, but also captivate us as all good stories
do. Even unbelievers have recognized for centuries that the
Bible is a treasure trove of stories. (Think of the many
movies, poems, plays, novels, paintings, and sculptures that
are based on the Scriptures.)

The Bible is full of sublime teaching—and sometimes
pathetic, sometimes amusing pictures of human failings. It
evokes tears and laughter, repulsion and admiration. To ask
questions about its content can, at the very least, provide
innocent amusement. Even better, asking questions can lead
us deeper into the content and make us appreciate and (it is
hoped) study more deeply this fascinating treasury of
stories.

This is not the first collection of questions and answers
about the Bible, and it probably will not be the last.
However, most previous books focused on the seriousness
of the text, neglecting the possibilities of finding things to

chuckle over and cry over. Too many of these volumes have been painfully dry.

I have tried to avoid dryness at all costs. The arrangement here is topical, with such topics as "Everyday Phrases from the Bible," "The Very Devil," "Whom Did God Ask?" "The Old Testament in the New," and "Supernatural Journeys." I hope the choice of topics will itself provide amusement. And the categories "Not to Be Taken Seriously" and "Curious Quotations" are just for laughs. One can't include *every* subject, of course, but the range is wide—miracles, churches, curses, Bible translations, authors, prophecies, demons, intertestamental writings, and many, many others. And while this volume of *The Best of Bible Trivia* focuses on the many interesting divine-human encounters in the Bible—and on the writing of the Bible itself—Volumes 1 and 2 cover many other subjects. In all, there are more than 1,500 questions arranged under more than 50 topical headings.

This book is made for browsing. It was made to fill up your time commuting on the train, waiting at the dentist's office, before dinner is on the table, on the freeway when you and the other two people in the backseat are in the mood for a game of "quiz me." In other words, the book is designed to be read randomly, anywhere, and with no preparation of any kind. It is designed to entertain the person who unashamedly likes to be entertained—and challenged.

The author would like to hear from any person who is able to correctly (and without peeking at the answers on the back of each page) answer every question in this book. In doing the research for this book, the author himself learned quite a bit, but not enough to answer every question correctly—at least, not yet.

Happy reading! I hope you enjoy getting better acquainted with the divine—and very human—Book of books.

PART 1
Dabbling with the Demonic

✦The Very Devil

1. According to Jude's epistle, who disputed with Satan over the body of Moses?
2. What animal does 1 Peter compare Satan to?
3. In what epistle does Paul refer to Satan as "the god of this world"?
4. What, according to the New Testament, is the final place for Satan?
5. In what Gospel does Jesus refer to Satan as "the prince of this world"?
6. What is Satan the father of?
7. What prophet spoke of the fallen Lucifer, usually taken to refer to Satan as a fallen angel?
8. According to the parable of the sower, what happens when someone hears the word of the kingdom and does not understand it?
9. According to John's Gospel, Satan was from the very beginning both a liar and a _____.
10. In what epistle does Paul call Satan the "spirit that worketh in the children of disobedience"?
11. What Gospel uses the name Beelzebub?
12. What book of the Bible speaks of the demonic fiend Abaddon and Apollyon, both names for Satan?
13. What apostle spoke of the contrast between Christ and Belial (presumably another name for the devil)?
14. What prophet spoke of "weeping for the king of Tyre" in a passage that has traditionally been interpreted as referring to Satan instead of a human king?

✦The Very Devil (Answers)

1. The archangel Michael (Jude 9)
2. A roaring lion (1 Peter 5:8)
3. 2 Corinthians (4:4)
4. A lake of fire and brimstone (Revelation 20:10)
5. John (14:30; 16:11)
6. Lies (John 8:44)
7. Isaiah (14:12)
8. The wicked one (Satan) snatches from the heart what was sown (Matthew 13:19)
9. A murderer (John 8:44)
10. Ephesians (2:2)
11. Matthew (12:24)
12. Revelation (9:11)
13. Paul (2 Corinthians 6:15)
14. Ezekiel (28:11-19)

15. In Luke's Gospel, Jesus refers to seeing the fall of Satan. What does he compare the fall to?
16. Who did Satan provoke to do a census in Israel?
17. What disciple did Satan enter into?
18. What disciple was told by Jesus that Satan wanted to sift him like wheat?
19. What New Testament man did Satan provoke to lie to the Holy Spirit?
20. Who had seven sons that were overcome by an evil spirit they were trying to cast out of a man?
21. What king of Israel was tormented by an evil spirit?
22. In the story of the demon-possessed boy healed by Jesus, what had the evil spirit been doing to the poor child?
23. What did the evil spirit do when Jesus cast him out of the man at Capernaum?
24. What possessed man ran around naked?
25. What was the affliction of the woman who had had an evil spirit for eighteen years?
26. What king had court prophets that had been the agents of a lying spirit?
27. What woman had Jesus driven seven demons out of?
28. In Revelation, for what reason do the demons perform miracles?
29. According to Jesus, when an evil spirit returns to a person, how many companions does it bring with it?
30. What does Satan masquerade as in the present world?

✦A Gallery of Gods

1. What fish-shaped god of the Philistines was disgraced when his statue was broken by the presence of the ark of the covenant?

15. Lightning (Luke 10:18)
16. David (1 Chronicles 21:1)
17. Judas Iscariot (Luke 22:3-4)
18. Peter (Luke 22:31)
19. Ananias (Acts 5:3)
20. Sceva (Acts 19:16)
21. Saul (1 Samuel 16:14-23)
22. Throwing him into the fire or water and making him foam at the mouth and grind his teeth (Mark 9:17-29)
23. Gave a loud scream (Mark 1:23-26)
24. The Gerasene demoniac (Luke 8:27)
25. She was bent and could not straighten up (Luke 13:11-16)
26. Ahab (1 Kings 22:2-22)
27. Mary Magdalene (Luke 8:2)
28. To bring the nations to war (Revelation 16:13-14)
29. Seven (Matthew 12:45)
30. An angel of light (2 Corinthians 11:14)

✦A Gallery of Gods (Answers)

1. Dagon (Judges 16:23; 1 Samuel 5:1-5; 1 Chronicles 10:10)

2. The Ammonites' bloodthirsty god was widely known in Israel because of the horrible practice of children being sacrificed to him. What was the name of this god?

3. The god of the Moabites also had child sacrifice as part of his worship. Solomon erected an altar for him, but Josiah tore it down. What was he called?

4. The people of Lystra were so dazzled by Paul and Barnabas that they called them by the name of two Greek gods. What were the names?

5. This fertility god of Canaan is mentioned more than any other foreign deity in the Bible. The prophet Elijah and, later, King Jehu of Israel, worked hard to stamp out his cult. What was his name?

6. This goddess of Canaan was associated with depraved worship practices. After Saul's death, his armor was placed in her temple by the Philistines. What was her name?

7. This Babylonian god is mentioned by Jeremiah as being filled with terror after the downfall of Babylon. What was his name?

8. This goddess of Asia had a magnificent temple in Ephesus, a city where Paul ran into trouble with some of her followers. Who was she?

9. In Paul's speech to the men of Athens, he mentions the altar of a god. What is the altar's inscription?

10. After Gideon's death, what Canaanite god did the Israelites turn to?

11. Ezekiel saw a woman weeping for what god?

12. Who worshiped Succoth-benoth?

13. What gods did the Avites worship?

14. What was the god of Ekron, consulted by King Ahaziah?

15. What was Nehushtan?

16. What god did the Sepharvites sacrifice their children to?

17. What nation was Milcom the god of?

18. While in the wilderness, what Moabite god did the Israelites begin to worship?

---

2. Moloch (Leviticus 18:21; 1 Kings 11:7; 2 Kings 23:10; Amos 5:26)
3. Chemosh (Numbers 21:29; 1 Kings 11:7; 2 Kings 23:13)
4. Zeus and Hermes (also called Jupiter and Mercury in some Bible translations) (Acts 14:12)
5. Baal (Judges 2:11; 1 Kings 16:32; 18:19; 19:18; 2 Kings 10:18)
6. Astaroth, or Ashtoreth (Judges 2:13; 1 Samuel 7:3; 31:10; 1 Kings 11:33; 2 Kings 23:13)
7. Marduk (Jeremiah 50:2)
8. Artemis (called Diana in some translations) (Acts 19:23—20:1)
9. "To an Unknown God" (Acts 17:22-23)
10. Baal-berith (Judges 8:33)
11. Tammuz (Ezekiel 8:14)
12. The Babylonians (2 Kings 17:30)
13. Nibhaz and Tartak (2 Kings 17:31)
14. Baal-zebub (2 Kings 1:2)
15. The brass serpent Moses had made, which the Israelites later worshiped as if it were a god (2 Kings 18:4)
16. Adrammelech (2 Kings 17:31)
17. Ammon (1 Kings 11:5)
18. Baal-peor (Numbers 25:1-3)

19. What god did Naaman the Syrian apologize to Elisha for worshiping?
20. What was the god of the men of Hamath?
21. What god did Amos say was symbolized by a star?
22. Who was King Sennacherib worshiping when his sons murdered him?
23. Whose ship had figures of the gods Castor and Pollux?
24. Who was the god of the men of Cuth?
25. What nation was Bel a god of?
26. What prophet mentions Nebo as one of the gods of Babylon?

◆Offerings to Idols

1. When Elijah challenged the priests of Baal, what were they sacrificing to their god?
2. What king of Israel offered sacrifices to the two golden calves he had made?
3. What idol, associated with Moses, was offered sacrifices by later generations?
4. What wicked king, a dabbler in sorcery, sacrificed his son in the fire?
5. What goddess did Jeremiah accuse the people of Judah of making sacrifices to?
6. What idol did the Israelites in the wilderness bring offerings to?
7. What people burnt their children as an offering to the gods Adrammelech and Anammelech?
8. What king despaired in the face of battle and offered his oldest son, the heir to the throne, as a sacrifice?
9. What wicked king of Judah built a Syrian style altar and offered up his son as a sacrifice?
10. What was the name of the foreign god that many Israelites had sacrificed their children to?

19. Rimmon (2 Kings 5:17-18)
20. Ashima (2 Kings 17:30)
21. Rephen (Amos 5:26—see Stephen's words in Acts 7:43)
22. Nisroch (2 Kings 19:36-37)
23. Paul's (Acts 28:11)
24. Nergal (2 Kings 17:30)
25. Babylonia (Jeremiah 51:44)
26. Isaiah (46:1)

✦Offerings to Idols (Answers)

1. A bullock (1 Kings 18:25)
2. Jeroboam (1 Kings 12:32-33)
3. The brazen serpent (2 Kings 18:4)
4. Manasseh (2 Kings 21:6)
5. The queen of heaven (Jeremiah 44:19)
6. The golden calf (Exodus 32:6)
7. The Sepharvites (2 Kings 17:31)
8. The king of Moab (2 Kings 3:26-27)
9. Ahaz (2 Chronicles 28:1-4, 23)
10. Molech (2 Kings 23:10)

PART 2
Encounters with the Divine

◆Encounters with Angels

1. The angel of the Lord appeared to the banished Hagar and told her what to name her child. What was the child's name?

2. How many angels rescued Lot and his family from the doomed city of Sodom?

3. What apostle was released from prison by an angel who opened the prison's iron gate?

4. The prophet Balaam could not see the Lord's angel, but his talking donkey could. What was it about the angel that made the donkey turn away?

5. Joshua encountered an angel who was captain of the host of the Lord. What was the angel's purpose in appearing to Joshua?

6. The angel of the Lord instructed Philip to go to Gaza. What person did Philip encounter afterward?

7. What was the name of the angel who appeared to Mary and to Zacharias?

8. This man's mother was visited by the angel of the Lord, who told her she would have a son who would be dedicated as a Nazarite. Who was he?

9. Elijah was nurtured by an angel after his flight from Israel's evil queen. Who was the queen?

10. Jacob is the only person known to have wrestled with an angel. What kindly act did the angel perform after the wrestling match?

11. What Roman official was visited by an angel who told him God had heard his prayers?

12. Who was commissioned by an angel to save Israel from the Midianites?

✦**Encounters with Angels** (Answers)

1. Ishmael (Genesis 16:1-12)
2. Two (Genesis 19:1-22)
3. Peter (Acts 12:1-19)
4. He was holding a drawn sword (Numbers 22:22-35)
5. To give him instructions on conquering Jericho (Joshua 5:13-15)
6. The Ethiopian eunuch (Acts 8:26-39)
7. Gabriel (Luke 1:5-38)
8. Samson (Judges 13:1-20)
9. Jezebel (1 Kings 19:1-8)
10. He blessed Jacob (Genesis 32:24-20)
11. Cornelius (Acts 10:1-8)
12. Gideon (Judges 6:11-23)

13. What kind of angelic beings guarded the entrance to Eden?
14. Who had his lips touched by a live coal held by a seraph?
15. What foreign army had 185,000 men killed by the angel of the Lord?
16. What person did an angel prevent from the act of child sacrifice?
17. What two guides did the angel of the Lord provide for the Israelites in the wilderness?
18. What ungodly ruler in New Testament times was struck down by an angel?
19. Who was carried by angels to Abraham's bosom?
20. What angel helped Daniel understand the future?
21. Who was told by an angel that the angel's name was a secret?
22. According to Revelation, what angel fights against Satan?
23. What kind of angels did Isaiah see in the temple praising God?
24. Who had a dream about an angel and goats?
25. What person saw the angel of the Lord in the form of a flame?
26. What prophet was fed two meals by an angel?
27. According to Jude, who fought with Satan over the body of Moses?
28. Where was Jesus when an angel came and strengthened him?
29. Where was Paul when an angel assured him that he would be tried before Caesar?
30. How many angels will be at the gates of the New Jerusalem?
31. According to Jesus, what causes the angels to rejoice?
32. Who had a vision of four angels holding the four winds of the earth?
33. Which Gospel says that an angel rolled away the stone from Jesus' tomb?
34. At the end time, what will an angel bind Satan with?

13. Cherubim (Genesis 3:24)
14. Isaiah (6:5-7)
15. The Assyrians (2 Kings 19:35)
16. Abraham (Genesis 22:11-18)
17. A pillar of fire and a pillar of cloud (Exodus 14:19-20)
18. Herod (Acts 12:23)
19. Lazarus (Luke 16:22)
20. Gabriel (Daniel 8:15-26; 9:21-27)
21. Samson's parents (Judges 13:17-18)
22. Michael (Revelation 12:7)
23. Seraphim (Isaiah 6:1-6)
24. Jacob (Genesis 31:11-12)
25. Moses (Exodus 3:1-22)
26. Elijah (1 Kings 19:5-8)
27. The archangel Michael (Jude 9)
28. Gethsemane (Luke 22:43)
29. On board ship during a storm (Acts 27:23-24)
30. Twelve (Revelation 21:12)
31. A repentant sinner (Luke 15:10)
32. John (Revelation 7:1)
33. Matthew (28:2)
34. A chain (Revelation 20:2)

35. How many angels pour out the bowls of wrath on the earth?
36. What prophet saw the Lord's angel riding on a red horse?
37. What is the name of the evil angel of the Abyss in Revelation?

◆A Book of Covenants

1. The covenant after the Flood was made not only between God and man, but also between God and the animals and the earth. What did God give as the sign of this covenant?
2. In God's covenant with Abraham, what ceremonial rite was made mandatory for all Abraham's male descendants?
3. In the covenant between God and Israel at Sinai, the agreement was broken almost immediately afterward by the Israelites. What did they do that was an infringement of the covenant?
4. According to Jeremiah's vision, where would the new covenant between God and man be written?
5. In the New Testament, a new covenant is instituted by Jesus. What does he use to symbolize this new covenant?

◆Who Asked God the Question?

1. "Why dost thou show me iniquity, and cause me to behold grievance?" (Hint: a prophet.)
2. "Why is my pain perpetual, and my wound incurable?" (Hint: a prophet.)
3. "Shall I go and smite these Philistines?" (Hint: a king.)

35. Seven (Revelation 16:1-21)
36. Zechariah (1:8)
37. Abaddon or Apollyon (Revelation 9:11)

✦A Book of Covenants (Answers)

1. A rainbow (Genesis 9:13)
2. Circumcision (Genesis 17:9-14)
3. They built and worshiped a graven image, the golden calf (Exodus 32)
4. On men's hearts (Jeremiah 31:33)
5. Wine, which symbolizes the blood of sacrifice (Mark 14:24)

✦Who Asked God the Question? (Answers)

1. Habakkuk (1:1-3)
2. Jeremiah (15:18)
3. David (1 Samuel 23:1-2)

4. "Am I my brother's keeper?" (Hint: you don't need one.)
5. "Lord, wilt thou slay also a righteous nation?" (Hint: a king.)
6. "Shall not the judge of all the earth do right?" (Hint: a patriarch.)
7. "Who am I, that I should go unto Pharaoh?"
8. "Ah, Lord God, wilt thou make a full end of the remnant of Israel?" (Hint: a prophet.)
9. "Behold, I am vile; what shall I answer thee?" (Hint: a righteous man.)
10. "Lord God, whereby shall I know that I inherit it?" (Hint: a patriarch.)
11. "Why is it that thou hast sent me?" (Hint: a leader and miracle worker.)
12. "Hast thou also brought evil upon the widow with whom I sojourn, by slaying her son?" (Hint: a prophet.)
13. "What wilt thou give me, seeing I go childless?" (Hint: a patriarch.)
14. "Shall one man sin and wilt thou be wroth with all the congregation?" (Hint: a leader and his brother.)
15. "Who is able to judge this thy so great a people?" (Hint: a king.)
16. "When I come unto the children of Israel and shall say unto them, The God of your fathers hath sent me unto you; and they shall say to me, What is his name? what shall I say to them?" (Hint: a leader.)
17. "Shall I pursue after this troop? shall I overtake them?" (Hint: a king.)
18. "Why is this come to pass, that there should today be one tribe lacking in Israel?" (Hint: a nation.)
19. "What shall I do unto this people? They are almost ready to stone me." (Hint: a leader.)
20. "Wherefore hast thou at all brought this people over Jordan, to deliver us into the hand of the Amorites, to destroy us?" (Hint: a leader.)

4. Cain (Genesis 4:9)
5. Abimelech (Genesis 20:4)
6. Abraham (Genesis 18:25)
7. Moses (Exodus 3:10-11)
8. Ezekiel (11:13)
9. Job (40:3-4)
10. Abram (Genesis 15:7-8)
11. Moses (Exodus 5:22)
12. Elijah (1 Kings 17:20)
13. Abraham (Genesis 15:2)
14. Moses and Aaron (Numbers 16:22)
15. Solomon (1 Kings 3:5-9)
16. Moses (Exodus 3:13)
17. David (1 Samuel 30:3-8)
18. The Israelites (Judges 21:2-3)
19. Moses (Exodus 17:3-4)
20. Joshua (7:7)

◆Whom Did God Ask?

1. "How long will this people provoke me?" (Hint: a leader.)
2. "Whom shall I send, and who will go for us?" (Hint: a prophet.)
3. "Have I any pleasure at all that the wicked should die?" (Hint: a prophet.)
4. "Doest thou well to be angry?" (Hint: a reluctant prophet.)
5. "Who told thee that thou wast naked?"
6. "Why is thy countenance fallen? If thou doest well, shalt thou not be accepted?" (Hint: a farmer.)
7. "How long wilt thou mourn for Saul, seeing I have rejected him from reigning over Israel?" (Hint: a judge and prophet.)
8. "I am the Lord, the God of all flesh; is there anything too hard for me?" (Hint: a prophet.)
9. "Son of man, can these bones live?" (Hint: a prophet.)
10. "Who is this that darkeneth counsel by words without knowledge?" (Hint: a righteous man.)
11. "Who hath made man's mouth?" (Hint: a leader.)
12. "What is this that thou hast done?" (Hint: a woman.)
13. "Shall the clay say to him that fashioneth it, What makest thou?" (Hint: a foreign king.)
14. "Shall seven years of famine come unto thee in thy land? Or wilt thou flee three months before thine enemies?" (Hint: a king.)
15. "Shall I not spare Nineveh, that great city?" (Hint: a prophet.)
16. "Hast thou an arm like God? Or canst thou thunder with a voice like him?" (Hint: a righteous man.)
17. "Why is this people of Jerusalem slidden back by a perpetual backsliding?" (Hint: a prophet.)
18. "Have not I commanded thee? Be strong and of a good courage; be not afraid." (Hint: a conqueror.)

✦Whom Did God Ask? (Answers)

1. Moses (Numbers 14:11)
2. Isaiah (6:8)
3. Ezekiel (18:23)
4. Jonah (4:9)
5. Adam (Genesis 3:11)
6. Cain (Genesis 4:6-7)
7. Samuel (1 Samuel 16:1)
8. Jeremiah (32:26-27)
9. Ezekiel (37:3)
10. Job (38:2)
11. Moses (Exodus 4:11)
12. Eve (Genesis 3:13)
13. Cyrus (Isaiah 45:1-9)
14. David (2 Samuel 24:13)
15. Jonah (4:11)
16. Job (40:9)
17. Jeremiah (8:4-12)
18. Joshua (1:1, 9)

19. "Is anything too hard for the Lord?" (Hint: a patriarch.)
20. "Hast thou killed, and also taken possession?" (Hint: a king.)

✦Visions of God

1. Who had a vision of the Ancient of Days seated upon a throne?
2. Who looked up steadfastly into heaven and saw Jesus on the right hand of God?
3. Who knew a man who had been caught up into the "third heaven"?
4. What seer described himself as "in the Spirit" when he received his visions?
5. What did Isaiah see filling the temple when he beheld God sitting on his throne?
6. Who saw the back of God, since he could not bear to see him face to face?
7. Who, besides Isaiah, saw the Lord sitting upon his throne?
8. What seer of weird visions beheld a throne like a sapphire?
9. Who saw a heavenly ladder with the Lord standing above it?
10. Who, along with Moses, saw God during the wilderness wanderings?

✦Ordained before Birth by God

1. What strongman was ordained before birth to deliver Israel from the Philistines?
2. What child, who later ministered with the priest Eli, was ordained before birth to serve God?

19. Abraham (Genesis 18:13)
20. Ahab (1 Kings 21:19)

✦Visions of God (Answers)

1. Daniel (7:9)
2. Stephen (Acts 7:55)
3. Paul (2 Corinthians 12:2)
4. John, author of Revelation (Revelation 4:2)
5. The train of God's robe (Isaiah 6:1)
6. Moses (Exodus 33:23)
7. The prophet Micaiah (2 Chronicles 18:18)
8. Ezekiel (1:26)
9. Jacob (Genesis 28:12-13)
10. Aaron, Nadab, Abihu, and seventy of the Israelite elders (Exodus 24:9-10)

✦Ordained before Birth by God (Answers)

1. Samson (Judges 13:2-5)
2. Samuel (1 Samuel 1:11-20)

3. What apostle was foreordained to minister to the Gentiles?
4. What kinsman of Christ was ordained to be his forerunner?
5. What Greek ruler's reign is usually considered to be predicted in the Book of Daniel?
6. What prophet was ordained before birth to be God's messenger?
7. What king of Judah had his birth and reign foretold to King Jeroboam?
8. What psalm, usually assumed to have been written by David, talks about God knowing him before his birth?
9. Who foretold Jesus' birth and ministry to Mary?

3. Paul (Galatians 1:15)
4. John the Baptist (Luke 1:13-17)
5. Alexander the Great (Daniel 11:2-4)
6. Jeremiah (1:5)
7. Josiah (1 Kings 13:2)
8. Psalm 139
9. The angel Gabriel (Luke 1:26-38)

PART 3
Miracles and Wonders

◆Supernatural Journeys

1. What prophet was able to travel for forty days on just the strength from a cake and water?
2. Elijah and Elisha walked across the Jordan River on dry ground after Elijah struck the waters with what?
3. Elijah outran a king's chariot, running all the way from Mount Carmel to Jezreel, almost ten miles. Who was the king?
4. How was Elijah taken up into heaven?
5. Israel crossed the Red Sea on dry ground and also crossed a river on dry ground. Which river?
6. What carried Philip from Gaza to Azotus?
7. What two people walked on water in the midst of a storm?
8. Who took Jesus to a pinnacle of the temple in Jerusalem?
9. Ezekiel was lifted up by a spirit, which held him between earth and heaven. What was the spirit holding on to?
10. Who was taken up into heaven in the sight of his followers?
11. What man knew someone who had been caught up to the third heaven?

◆Moses and Miracles

1. What did Moses mount on a pole as a way for healing the ailing Israelites?
2. What bird served as miracle food for the Israelites?

◆Supernatural Journeys (Answers)

1. Elijah (1 Kings 19:5-8)
2. His mantle (2 Kings 2:8)
3. Ahab (1 Kings 18:41-46)
4. In a whirlwind (2 Kings 2:11)
5. The Jordan (Joshua 3)
6. The Spirit of the Lord (Acts 8:39-40)
7. Jesus and Peter (Matthew 14:22-32)
8. The devil (Matthew 4:5-7)
9. A lock of Ezekiel's hair (Ezekiel 8:1-3)
10. Jesus (Acts 1:9)
11. Paul (2 Corinthians 12:1-7)

◆Moses and Miracles (Answers)

1. A brass serpent (Numbers 21:5-9)
2. Quail (Exodus 16:11-13)

3. What did Moses do to bring forth water from the rock at Kadesh?
4. What animal came forth out of the Nile in droves?
5. What miraculous thing happened to Moses' hand?
6. What was the unique feature of the hailstorm that God sent upon the Egyptians?
7. What did Moses' staff turn into?
8. What everyday substance was changed into a plague of lice?
9. What caused the boils on the Egyptians?
10. What did the Nile waters turn into?
11. What plague was sent upon the Egyptians' cattle?
12. Who appeared on the Mount of Transfiguration with Moses and Jesus?
13. What did Moses cast into the bitter water at Marah to make it sweet?
14. What happened to Aaron's staff when placed in the Tent of Meeting?
15. What was done to stop the plague that killed 14,700 of the Israelites?
16. What voracious insect was a plague on the Egyptian flora?
17. What happened to the rebellious Korah and his men?
18. What happened to 250 men who offered incense?
19. For how long did the thick darkness hang over the Egyptians?
20. What substance, called bread from heaven, fed the Israelites in the wilderness?
21. What hid the departing Israelites?
22. Who was made leprous and then healed after her rebellious acts?
23. What did the Israelites put on their doorposts so the angel of death would pass over?
24. What did the Lord use to part the Red Sea?
25. What means did the Lord use to halt the Egyptian chariots?
26. What happened to the manna the Israelites tried to hoard?

3. He struck it twice (Numbers 20:1-11)
4. Frogs (Exodus 8:5-7)
5. It became leprous, then became normal again (Exodus 4:7)
6. It was accompanied by fire that ran along the ground (Exodus 9:22-26)
7. A serpent (Exodus 4:2-4)
8. Dust (Exodus 8:16-17)
9. Ashes that were turned into dust (Exodus 9:8-12)
10. Blood (Exodus 7:19-25)
11. Murrain (Exodus 9:1-7)
12. Elijah (Luke 9:28-36)
13. A tree (Exodus 15:23-25)
14. It sprouted and blossomed and bore almonds (Numbers 17)
15. An offering of incense was made (Numbers 16:46-50)
16. Locusts (Exodus 10:12-15)
17. They were swallowed up by the earth (Numbers 16:28-33)
18. They were consumed by fire from the Lord (Numbers 16:16-18)
19. Three days (Exodus 10:21-23)
20. Manna (Exodus 16:14-15)
21. A cloud (Exodus 14:19-20)
22. Miriam (Numbers 12)
23. Lamb's blood (Exodus 12:21-30)
24. A strong east wind (Exodus 14:21)
25. He made their wheels come off (Exodus 14:23-25)
26. It was filled with maggots (Exodus 16:20)

27. Who was slain by the angel of death?
28. What was Moses supposed to do to the rock at Horeb to bring water from it?
29. What consumed the offering on the altar?
30. What did Moses do at Taberah when the fire of the Lord destroyed many Israelites?
31. What brought the locust plague to a halt?
32. When the plague of hail came, where was the one place it did not fall?
33. Whose rod was turned into a serpent that swallowed the Egyptian sorcerers' serpents?
34. What bit the Israelites, causing Moses to fix a brass figure on a pole?

◆Wonders of Elijah and Elisha

1. What happened to the children who made fun of Elisha's bald head?
2. Who did Elijah supply meal and oil for through miraculous means?
3. What did the bones of Elisha do to a dead man?
4. What did Elisha do to make an ax head float to the surface of the water?
5. Who was healed of leprosy when he followed Elisha's instructions?
6. Who appeared with Jesus and Elijah on the Mount of Transfiguration?
7. What birds fed Elijah in the wilderness?
8. What river did Elijah part by striking it with his mantle?
9. What did Elisha do to make the poisoned pottage edible?
10. What happened to the Syrian soldiers when Elisha prayed?
11. How long was rain withheld after Elijah's prayer?

27. The firstborn among the Egyptians (Exodus 12:29-30)
28. Strike it (Exodus 17:1-6)
29. Fire from the Lord (Leviticus 9:22-24)
30. He prayed and the fire died down (Numbers 11:1-2)
31. The Lord blew them away with a strong west wind (Exodus 10:16-20)
32. In Goshen, where the Israelites dwelled (Exodus 9:26)
33. Aaron's (Exodus 7:10-12)
34. Fiery serpents (Numbers 21:5-9)

◆Wonders of Elijah and Elisha (Answers)

1. They were torn apart by two bears (2 Kings 2:23-25)
2. A widow and her son (1 Kings 17:13-16)
3. Brought him back to life (2 Kings 13:20-21)
4. He threw a stick into the water (2 Kings 6:4-7)
5. Naaman the Syrian (2 Kings 5:1-14)
6. Moses (Luke 9:28-36)
7. Ravens (1 Kings 17:2-7)
8. The Jordan (2 Kings 2:8)
9. He poured meal into it (2 Kings 4:38-41)
10. They were struck blind (2 Kings 6:18)
11. Three and a half years (1 Kings 17:1)

12. Who conceived a son after Elisha predicted she would?

13. What did Elijah call on to destroy the soldiers sent to arrest him?

14. Who was Elijah up against when fire from the Lord burned up a sacrifice and the water around the altar?

15. How many men did Elisha feed with twenty loaves of barley and some ears of corn?

16. How did Elisha raise the Shunammite woman's son from the dead?

17. What did Elisha's servant see after Elisha prayed that his eyes would be opened?

18. For whom did Elisha supply water miraculously?

19. What took Elijah into heaven?

20. Who fed Elijah after he prayed to the Lord to take his life?

21. What did Elisha do for the Syrian soldiers after leading them to Samaria?

22. What did Elisha supply the poor widow with?

23. How did Elisha purify the bitter water?

24. Who did Elijah miraculously outrun on the way to Jezreel?

◆Miracles of Jesus

1. How was the woman with the issue of blood healed by Jesus?

2. What woman got up and started doing household chores after Jesus healed her of a fever?

3. What unproductive tree did Jesus wither by cursing it?

4. Where did Jesus work his first miracle?

5. Who appeared with Jesus at his miraculous Transfiguration?

6. Which apostle did Jesus enable to walk (briefly) on water?

12. The Shunammite woman (2 Kings 4:14-17)
13. Fire from heaven (2 Kings 1:10-12)
14. The prophets of Baal (1 Kings 18:17-38)
15. A hundred (2 Kings 4:42-44)
16. He stretched his body out on the boy's (2 Kings 4:32-37)
17. An angelic army (2 Kings 6:15-17)
18. The armies of the kings of Judah, Israel, and Edom (2 Kings 3:14-20)
19. A whirlwind (2 Kings 2:11)
20. An angel (1 Kings 19:4-8)
21. Prayed for the healing of their blindness (2 Kings 6:19-20)
22. Large quantities of oil (2 Kings 4:1-7)
23. He threw a container of salt into it (2 Kings 2:19-22)
24. Ahab (1 Kings 18:46)

◆Miracles of Jesus (Answers)

1. She touched the hem of his garment (Matthew 9:20-22)
2. Peter's mother-in-law (Matthew 8:14-15)
3. A fig tree (Matthew 21:17-20)
4. Cana (John 2:1-11)
5. Elijah and Moses (Matthew 17:1-9)
6. Peter (Matthew 14:28-31)

7. What disciples did Jesus call after blessing them with an enormous catch of fish?

8. Who did Jesus send to catch a fish that had a coin in its mouth?

9. When Jesus healed the blind man of Bethsaida, what did the man say people looked like?

10. What widow had her dead son brought to life by Jesus?

11. Where was Jesus when he healed the son of an official from Capernaum?

12. What was the affliction of the man Jesus healed by sending him to the pool of Siloam?

13. Why did the people complain when Jesus healed a woman who had been stooped for eighteen years?

14. Where was Jesus when he miraculously escaped from a crowd that was going to push him off a cliff?

15. What was the other affliction of the deaf man Jesus healed in the Decapolis?

16. How many loaves of bread were used to feed the five thousand?

17. How was Joseph told about Jesus' miraculous conception?

18. Who announced Jesus' conception to Mary?

19. What was the affliction of the man Jesus healed after his famous Sermon on the Mount?

20. What little girl did Jesus raise from the dead after telling people she was only asleep?

21. What did Jesus say to calm the storm on the lake?

22. When Jesus healed a man of dumbness, what did the Pharisees accuse him of?

23. When Jesus healed a paralyzed man, what did the man pick up and carry home?

24. When Jesus healed ten lepers, how many came back to thank him?

25. How many loaves did Jesus use to feed the four thousand?

7. Peter, James, and John (Luke 5:4-11)
8. Peter (Matthew 17:24-27)
9. Like trees walking (Mark 8:22-26)
10. The widow of Nain (Luke 7:11-15)
11. Cana (John 4:46-54)
12. Blindness (John 9:1-7)
13. He healed her on the Sabbath (Luke 13:11-13)
14. His hometown, Nazareth (Luke 4:29-30)
15. Almost mute (Mark 7:31-35)
16. Five (Matthew 14:15-21)
17. In a dream (Matthew 1:18-21)
18. The angel Gabriel (Luke 1:26-38)
19. Leprosy (Matthew 8:1-4)
20. Jairus's daughter (Matthew 9:23-25)
21. "Peace, be still!" (Matthew 8:23-27)
22. Having demonic power (Matthew 9:34)
23. His bed (Matthew 9:1-8)
24. One (Luke 17:11-19)
25. Seven (Matthew 15:32-39)

26. What woman had her daughter healed, even after Jesus told her that he had been sent to the Jews, not to foreigners?
27. Which Gospel records the miraculous catch of fish after Jesus' resurrection?
28. Which apostle cut off a man's ear at Jesus' arrest, and then watched Jesus heal the ear?
29. In what town did Jesus heal a demon-possessed man in the synagogue?
30. What man of Bethany did Jesus bring back to life?
31. Which Gospel records the ability of the resurrected Jesus to walk through locked doors?
32. What was the affliction of the man Jesus healed on the Sabbath at the home of a Pharisee?
33. What Roman of Capernaum asked that Jesus heal his servant?
34. When Jesus was healing people, what prophet's writings did he claim to be fulfilling?
35. Where did Jesus send the demons he drove out of the Gadarene demoniacs?
36. According to Matthew's Gospel, what Sabbath healing caused the Pharisees to plot to kill Jesus?
37. What did Jesus tell the two blind men not to do after he healed them?
38. What future disciple did Jesus see, through miraculous means, sitting under a fig tree?
39. When Jesus healed a man who was both blind and dumb, what demon did the Pharisees accuse him of consorting with?
40. When the disciples saw Jesus walking on the water, what did they think he was?
41. What was the affliction of the young boy who was throwing himself into the fire?
42. How did Jesus heal the two blind men who asked for his help?
43. Where was Jesus doing his healing work when he caused the chief priests and the scribes to be angry?

26. The Canaanite woman (Matthew 15:22-28)
27. John (21:3-11)
28. Peter (Luke 22:49-51)
29. Capernaum (Luke 4:31-37)
30. Lazarus (John 11)
31. John (20:19-21)
32. Dropsy (Luke 14:1-4)
33. The centurion (Matthew 8:5-13)
34. Isaiah (Matthew 8:17)
35. Into a herd of pigs (Matthew 8:28-34)
36. The healing of the man with the withered hand (Matthew 12:10-14)
37. Not to tell anyone else (Matthew 9:27-31)
38. Nathanael (John 1:48)
39. Beelzebub (Matthew 12:24)
40. A ghost (Mark 6:45-50)
41. He was demon-possessed (Matthew 17:14-18)
42. He touched their eyes (Matthew 20:30-34)
43. In the temple (Matthew 21:14-16)

44. What miracle in Jesus' life is mentioned most in the New Testament?
45. Where did Jesus heal a man who had been sick for 38 years?

✦Miracles of Paul and Peter

1. What dead man at Troas was raised up by Paul after falling out of a window?
2. Who did Peter heal of long-term palsy?
3. Where did Paul exorcise a spirit from a possessed girl, whose owners then became furious?
4. What woman did Peter raise from the dead?
5. Where did Paul heal a crippled man?
6. Who, with Peter, healed a crippled man at the Beautiful Gate?
7. What sorcerer was blinded at Paul's command?
8. What, placed on Paul's body, brought about healings and exorcisms?
9. On what island did Paul heal the governor's family and many other people?
10. What miraculous occurrence delivered Paul and Silas from prison in Philippi?
11. What happened when Peter and John placed their hands on the believers at Samaria?
12. What part of Peter was supposed to produce healings?
13. What happened when Paul placed his hands on the believers at Ephesus?
14. What dangerous creature did not affect Paul when it bit him?
15. How many times was Peter delivered from prison by an angel?

44. His resurrection
45. The pool at Bethesda (John 4:46-54)

✦Miracles of Paul and Peter (Answers)

1. Eutychus (Acts 20:9-10)
2. Aeneas (Acts 9:33-34)
3. Philippi (Acts 16:16-18)
4. Dorcas (Acts 9:36-41)
5. Lystra (Acts 14:8-10)
6. John (Acts 3:1-6)
7. Elymas (Acts 13:8-11)
8. Aprons and handkerchiefs (Acts 19:11-12)
9. Malta (Acts 28:8-9)
10. An earthquake (Acts 16:25-33)
11. They received the Holy Spirit (Acts 8:14-17)
12. His shadow (Acts 5:15-16)
13. They spoke in tongues and proclaimed the gospel (Acts 19:1-7)
14. A viper (Acts 28:3-6)
15. Twice (Acts 5:17-29; 12:1-17)

✦Working Wonders with Water

1. Who made an ax head float on the water?
2. Who walked on the Sea of Galilee?
3. What did Moses do to heal the bitter waters of Marah?
4. Who was healed of leprosy after dipping seven times in the Jordan?
5. What judge wrung out a bowlful of water from a fleece in answer to prayer?
6. What river was turned into blood?
7. Who healed Jericho's water supply by throwing salt into it?
8. Who turned water into wine?
9. Who died when the parted Red Sea became unparted?
10. When the Israelites in the wilderness complained about lack of water, where did the water come from?
11. How did God water the thirsty army of Israel?
12. Who calmed the sea by speaking to it?
13. Who parted the Jordan by striking it with his mantle?
14. What were the Israelite priests carrying when they crossed the Jordan on dry ground?

✦Supernatural Fire

1. What two sinful cities were destroyed by fire and brimstone from heaven?
2. When the Israelites were wandering in the wilderness, what did they follow by night?
3. According to Daniel, this astonishing person had a throne like a fire of flame? Who was he?
4. What did the seraph touch the trembling Isaiah's tongue with?

✦Working Wonders with Water (Answers)

1. Elisha (2 Kings 2:19-22)
2. Jesus and Peter (Matthew 14:25-31)
3. He cast a tree into the waters (Exodus 15:23-25)
4. Naaman the Syrian (2 Kings 5:14)
5. Gideon (Judges 6:38)
6. The Nile (Exodus 7:20)
7. Elisha (2 Kings 2:19-22)
8. Jesus (John 2:1-10)
9. The Egyptians (Exodus 14:21-29)
10. A rock (Exodus 17:1-6; 20:1-11)
11. He ordered them to dig trenches, and in the morning they were filled with water (2 Kings 3:14-22)
12. Jesus (Mark 4:39)
13. Elijah (2 Kings 2:8-14)
14. The ark of the covenant (Joshua 3:7-17)

✦Supernatural Fire (Answers)

1. Sodom and Gomorrah (Genesis 19:24)
2. A pillar of fire (Exodus 13:21)
3. The Ancient of Days (Daniel 7:9)
4. A live coal from the altar (Isaiah 6:6)

5. According to Revelation, where is the place reserved for those whose names are not in the book of life?
6. What did the cherubim use to guard the entrance to Eden?
7. How did God first appear to Moses?
8. What strange phenomenon accompanied the plague of hail in Egypt?
9. What mountain did the Lord descend upon in fire?
10. What two sons of Aaron were devoured by fire for making an improper offering to the Lord?
11. How did God deal with the Israelites who were complaining about their misfortunes in the wilderness?
12. What judge of Israel was visited by an angel, whose staff caused meat and bread to be consumed by fire?
13. How did Elijah respond to an army captain's summons to present himself to King Ahaziah?
14. What two men saw a chariot of fire drawn by horses of fire?
15. Where, in answer to Elijah's prayer, did fire from the Lord consume both the sacrifice and the altar?

✦Battles Won Supernaturally

1. What prophet's word caused the Syrian soldiers to be struck blind?
2. What nation's army was destroyed in the Red Sea?
3. What nation was Israel fighting when Moses' arms, held aloft, caused Israel to win?
4. What weather phenomenon did the Lord use to defeat the Amorites when Joshua and his men were fighting them?
5. What army was defeated when an angel of the Lord struck down 185,000 soldiers?
6. When Samuel was offering a sacrifice, what did the Lord do to rattle the Philistines?

5. A lake of fire and brimstone (Revelation 20)
6. A flaming sword (Genesis 3:24)
7. In a burning bush that was not consumed (Exodus 3:2)
8. Fire that ran along the ground (Exodus 9:23)
9. Sinai (Exodus 19:18)
10. Nadab and Abihu (Leviticus 10:1-2)
11. His fire devoured them (Numbers 11:1-3)
12. Gideon (Judges 6:21)
13. He called down fire from heaven on the captain and his men (2 Kings 1:9-12)
14. Elijah and Elisha (2 Kings 2:11)
15. Mount Carmel (1 Kings 18:16-40)

✦Battles Won Supernaturally (Answers)

1. Elisha's (2 Kings 6:18-23)
2. Egypt (Exodus 14:13-31)
3. Amalek (Exodus 17:11)
4. Large hailstones (Joshua 10:6-13)
5. Assyria's (2 Kings 19:35)
6. Thundered from heaven (1 Samuel 7:10)

7. What occurred when Jonathan and his armor-bearer attacked the Philistines?
8. What made the Syrians flee, thinking the Israelites had joined forces with Egyptians and Hittites?
9. Who were the Judeans fighting when God helped them slaughter a half million soldiers?
10. What king led the people in singing and praising God, leading God to destroy the armies of the Ammonites, Moabites, and Edomites?

7. An earthquake (1 Samuel 14:11-15)
8. The Lord made a sound like a thundering army (2 Kings 7:6-7)
9. Israel (2 Chronicles 13:15-16)
10. Jehoshaphat (2 Chronicles 20:22)

PART 4
Sacred Places and Acts

✦Houses of Worship

1. What gruesome object did the Philistines fasten in the temple of Dagon?
2. Which goddess had a notorious temple at Ephesus?
3. Why did John not see a temple in the New Jerusalem?
4. Whose temple did Abimelech burn while the people of Shechem were hiding inside?
5. Who received a vision of the Jerusalem temple while he was in exile in Babylon?
6. According to Paul, who is called to be the temple of God?
7. What Assyrian emperor was assassinated by his sons while he was worshiping in his pagan temple?
8. Who was told in a vision to measure the temple in Jerusalem?
9. Who carried away furnishings from the Jerusalem temple and put them in the temple at Babylon?
10. What was Jesus talking about when he spoke of destroying the temple and raising it up in three days?
11. What holy object was taken by the Philistines into the temple of Dagon, causing Dagon's image to fall down?
12. Who built the first temple in Jerusalem?
13. Who built a temple for Baal in Samaria?
14. After Saul's death, where did the Philistines carry his armor?
15. Who asked Elisha's forgiveness for worshiping in the temple of the god Rimmon?

✦Houses of Worship (Answers)

1. Saul's head (1 Chronicles 10:10)
2. Diana (or Artemis) (Acts 19:27-28)
3. God and the Lamb are the temple (Revelation 21:22)
4. The temple of the god Berith (Judges 9:46-49)
5. Ezekiel (40-42)
6. All believers (1 Corinthians 6:19)
7. Sennacherib (2 Kings 19:37)
8. John (Revelation 11:1-2)
9. Nebuchadnezzar (2 Chronicles 36:7)
10. His body (John 2:19-21)
11. The ark of the covenant (1 Samuel 5:2-4)
12. Solomon (1 Kings 6)
13. Ahab (1 Kings 16:32)
14. The temple of Ashtoreth (1 Samuel 31:10)
15. Naaman the Syrian (2 Kings 5:18)

16. What king issued an order allowing the Jews to rebuild the temple in Jerusalem?
17. Who was taken to the highest point of the Jerusalem temple?
18. What king tricked the followers of Baal by gathering them in Baal's temple and then slaughtering them?
19. Who had an Assyrian-style altar made for the Jerusalem temple?
20. Who did Solomon hire to take charge of building the temple?

◆Horns of the Altar

1. Who built the first altar?
2. What military leader was killed while holding on to the horns of the altar?
3. What book of the Bible mentions a talking altar?
4. Who almost sacrificed his much-loved son on an altar, but was stopped by an angel?
5. What king of Judah tore down Jeroboam's altar at Bethel and pounded the stones into dust?
6. Who built an altar and called it "The Lord is my banner"?
7. What kind of stone was, according to the Law, not supposed to be used in making an altar?
8. What was the altar in the tabernacle made of?
9. Which of the twelve tribes caused civil war when they built a magnificent altar on the banks of the Jordan?
10. What judge built an altar and called it "The Lord is peace"?
11. What king of Israel built a Baal altar to please his pagan wife?
12. What judge's parents saw an angel going up to heaven in the flames on the altar?

16. Darius (Ezra 6:1-12)
17. Jesus (Matthew 4:5)
18. Jehu of Israel (2 Kings 10:18-27)
19. King Ahaz (2 Kings 16:10-17)
20. Hiram of Tyre (1 Kings 7:13-14)

✦Horns of the Altar (Answers)

1. Noah (Genesis 8:20)
2. Joab (1 Kings 2:28-34)
3. Revelation (16:7)
4. Abraham (Genesis 22:9)
5. Josiah (2 Kings 23:15)
6. Moses (Exodus 17:15)
7. Cut stones (Exodus 20:25)
8. Acacia wood covered with bronze (Exodus 27:1)
9. Reuben, Gad, and part of Manasseh (Joshua 22:1)
10. Gideon (Judges 6:24)
11. Ahab (1 Kings 16:32)
12. Samson's (Judges 13:20)

13. What judge and prophet built an altar to the Lord at Ramah?
14. What king was told to built an altar in a threshing place?
15. What rebellious son of David sought refuge from Solomon by holding on to the horns of the altar?
16. Who took bones out of tombs and burned them on an altar to defile it?
17. Who had a vision of the Lord standing beside the altar?
18. What king of Israel changed the religious institutions of the country by building an altar at Bethel?
19. What good king's birth was foretold hundreds of years before the fact by a prophet standing before the altar at Bethel?
20. What happened to Jeroboam's altar when he ordered his men to seize a prophet in front of it?
21. What leader was told to tear down his father's altar to Baal?
22. What god's priests danced around the altar while they cut themselves with knives and daggers?
23. What prophet triumphed when God consumed the offering on the altar and shamed the prophets of Baal?
24. What priest of Judah placed a money box near the temple's altar?
25. Who built an altar and named it for El, the God of Israel?
26. What evil king of Judah built an altar modeled on the altars of Syria?
27. Who rebuilt the Jerusalem altar when the exiles returned to Israel?
28. Who had his lips touched by a coal from the altar in the temple?
29. What prophet had a vision of an idol near the altar of God?
30. What prophet foresaw the destruction of the altars of Bethel?

13. Samuel (1 Samuel 7:17)
14. David (2 Samuel 24:18)
15. Adonijah (1 Kings 1:50)
16. Josiah (2 Kings 23:16)
17. Amos (9:1)
18. Jeroboam (1 Kings 12:32)
19. Josiah's (1 Kings 13:2)
20. It fell apart and the ashes scattered (1 Kings 13:5)
21. Gideon (Judges 6:25)
22. Baal's (1 Kings 18:26-29)
23. Elijah (1 Kings 18)
24. Jehoiada (2 Kings 12:9)
25. Jacob (Genesis 33:20)
26. Ahaz (2 Kings 16:10)
27. The priest Joshua (Ezra 3:2)
28. Isaiah (6:6)
29. Ezekiel (8:5)
30. Amos (3:14)

31. Who constructed the first altar covered with gold?
32. What prophet spoke of the Jews weeping and wailing in front of the altar because God would not accept their offerings?
33. What patriarch built an altar after he arrived in Canaan for the first time?
34. What priest saw an angel standing beside the incense altar?
35. Where did Paul see an altar inscribed "To an Unknown God"?
36. Who had a vision of the souls of the martyrs underneath the altar?
37. Who told people to make peace with their brothers before they made a sacrifice on the altar?
38. In what book does the Lord tell Moses to tear down all the pagan altars he finds?
39. What priest led a movement in which the people tore down the Baal altars and killed Mattan, the priest of Baal?
40. What wicked king of Judah built altars for the worship of Baal and the stars?

◆Speaking of Churches

1. What church was neither hot nor cold?
2. What church began in the home of Lydia, the seller of purple?
3. At what church was Paul accused of turning the world upside down?
4. What church had two bickering women named Euodia and Syntyche?
5. In what church did Paul raise up Eutychus, who had fallen to his death out of a window?
6. What church was the scene of a burning of wicked books?

31. Solomon (1 Kings 6:20)
32. Malachi (2:13)
33. Abraham (Genesis 12:7)
34. Zacharias (Luke 1:11)
35. Athens (Acts 17:23)
36. John (Revelation 6:9)
37. Jesus (Matthew 5:24)
38. Exodus (34:13)
39. Jehoiada (2 Kings 11:18)
40. Manasseh (2 Kings 21:3-5)

✦Speaking of Churches (Answers)

1. Laodicea (Revelation 3:15-16)
2. Philippi (Acts 16:15, 40)
3. Thessalonica (Acts 17:6)
4. Philippi (Philippians 4:1-3)
5. Troas (Acts 20:7-12)
6. Ephesus (Acts 19:19)

7. At what church were believers first called Christians?
8. Who founded the church at Colossae?
9. What church had a false prophetess named Jezebel as a member?
10. Who visited the church at Babylon?
11. What church suffered because of the "synagogue of Satan"?
12. What member of the Colossian church received a letter from Paul?
13. What church received epistles from two different apostles?
14. At what church did Paul preach his first recorded sermon?
15. What church had a former demon-possessed girl as a member?
16. What was the first church to appoint deacons?
17. Who helped Paul establish the church in Corinth?
18. What church tolerated the heresy of the Nicolaitans?
19. What churches had fallen prey to the legalistic Judaizers?
20. What is the most commended church in Revelation?
21. What church received from Paul an epistle that has never been found?
22. What church took up a large love offering for the needy believers in Jerusalem?
23. On what Greek island did Titus supervise the churches?
24. What church saw the martyrdom of faithful Antipas?
25. What was the first church to send forth missionaries?
26. What church was Silas from?
27. What love-filled church sent members to accompany Paul all the way to Athens?
28. What church was noted for hating the Nicolaitan heresy?
29. To what church did Jesus say, "Behold, I stand at the door and knock"?
30. At what church did believers hold their property in common?

7. Antioch (Acts 11:26)
8. Epaphras (Colossians 1:7)
9. Thyatira (Revelation 2:18-29)
10. Peter (1 Peter 5:13)
11. Smyrna (Revelation 2:8-11)
12. Philemon
13. Ephesus (the Letter to the Ephesians from Paul and Revelation 2:1-7 from John)
14. Antioch of Pisidia (Acts 13:16)
15. Philippi (Acts 16:18)
16. Jerusalem (Acts 6:1-7)
17. Priscilla and Aquila (Acts 18:2)
18. Pergamos (Revelation 2:12-17)
19. The churches of Galatia (Galatians 1:6-9)
20. Philadelphia (Revelation 3:7-13)
21. Laodicea (Colossians 4:16)
22. Antioch (Acts 11:30)
23. Crete (Titus 1:5)
24. Pergamum (Revelation 2:13)
25. Jerusalem (Acts 8:5, 14)
26. Antioch (Acts 15:34)
27. Berea (Acts 17:10-15)
28. Ephesus (Revelation 2:6)
29. Laodicea (Revelation 3:20)
30. Jerusalem (Acts 2:44-45)

31. Who was sent by the Jerusalem church to oversee the church at Antioch?
32. To what church did Paul send Epaphroditus as a minister?
33. What church began at Pentecost?
34. What church had Crispus, a synagogue leader, as a member?
35. Where did Paul have a vision asking him to found churches in Europe?
36. At what church were Paul and Barnabas set apart by the Holy Spirit to do missionary work?
37. Who reported his vision of unclean animals to the church at Jerusalem?
38. At what church did Paul have a "loyal yokefellow"?
39. At what church did some people follow the teachings of Balaam?
40. What church was told by John to buy white clothing to hide its nakedness?
41. At what church did the Egyptian-born Apollos first serve?
42. What church did Timothy grow up in?
43. What apostle was supposed to be the rock on which the church was built?
44. Who founded the church at Antioch of Pisidia?
45. From what Asian church was Paul driven out by unbelieving Jews?
46. What church was overseen by James?
47. In what church were Christians guilty of taking other Christians to court?
48. Who established the church at Ephesus?

✦Baptisms

1. What magician came to be baptized by Philip?
2. Who referred to the Israelites crossing of the Red Sea as a baptism?

31. Barnabas (Acts 11:22)
32. Philippi (Philippians 2:25)
33. Jerusalem (Acts 2:47)
34. Corinth (Acts 18:8)
35. Troas (Acts 16:9)
36. Antioch (Acts 13:2)
37. Peter (Acts 11:1-18)
38. Philippi (Philippians 4:3)
39. Pergamum (Revelation 2:14)
40. Laodicea (Revelation 3:18)
41. Ephesus (Acts 18:24-28)
42. Lystra (Acts 16:1)
43. Peter (Matthew 16:18)
44. Paul (Acts 13:14)
45. Iconium (Acts 14:5)
46. Jerusalem (Acts 15:13)
47. Corinth (1 Corinthians 6:1-4)
48. Paul (Acts 18:19; 19:1-10)

✦Baptisms (Answers)

1. Simon the sorceror (Acts 8:12-13)
2. Paul (1 Corinthians 10:1-2)

3. What tradeswoman was baptized by Paul and Silas?

4. How many people were baptized on the day of Pentecost?

5. Who baptized Paul?

6. What Roman official did Peter baptize?

7. What kind of baptism did John promise the Christ would administer?

8. What foreign dignitary did Philip baptize?

9. What man of Philippi took Paul and Silas home and was baptized by them?

10. In what city did Crispus, the synagogue ruler, believe Paul's message and submit to baptism?

11. Where did Paul baptize twelve men who had received the baptism of John?

12. Which Gospel opens with John the Baptist preaching in the desert?

13. In which Gospel does John try to dissuade Jesus from being baptized?

14. What did John the Baptist tell the tax collectors who came to him for baptism?

15. Which epistle mentions "one Lord, one faith, one baptism"?

16. Which epistles compare baptism to burial?

17. Which epistle says that the flood waters at the time of Noah symbolize baptism?

✦The Anointed Ones

1. Who anointed a stone and dedicated it to God?

2. What holy man was anointed by an immoral woman?

3. What substance was usually used for anointing in Israel?

4. Who, according to James, should anoint the sick believer with oil?

5. Who did Moses anoint with the blood of a ram?

3. Lydia (Acts 16:14-15)
4. About 3,000 (Acts 2:41)
5. Ananias (Acts 9:18)
6. Cornelius (Acts 10:23-48)
7. A baptism with the Holy Spirit and with fire (John 3:16)
8. The Ethiopian eunuch (Acts 8:38)
9. The jailor (Acts 16:26-33)
10. Corinth (Acts 18:8)
11. Ephesus (Acts 19:1-7)
12. Mark
13. Matthew (3:13-15)
14. Not to collect any more than was legal (Luke 3:12-13)
15. Ephesians (4:5)
16. Romans (6:4) and Colossians (2:12)
17. Hebrews (3:17-22)

✦The Anointed Ones (Answers)

1. Jacob (Genesis 28:18)
2. Jesus (Luke 7:38)
3. Olive oil
4. The church elders (James 5:14)
5. Aaron and his sons (Leviticus 8:23)

6. What New Testament word means "anointed"?
7. What revered judge anointed Saul?
8. What priest anointed Solomon king?
9. Who was anointed by the Holy Spirit?
10. What Persian king was considered to be God's anointed one?
11. What Old Testament word means "anointed"?
12. What apostle told the early Christians that all believers were anointed by the Holy Spirit?
13. Who anointed the tabernacle with oil?
14. What leader anointed David as king?
15. What person was, prior to his fall, anointed by God?
16. Where did the men of Judah gather to anoint David as their king?

◆Healthy Confessions

1. What wicked king of Judah confessed his sins when he was taken into captivity in Assyria?
2. Who confessed to God that he had done wrong in taking a census of Israel?
3. Who confessed his denial of Jesus?
4. What sneaky Israelite confessed that he had stolen goods from fallen Jericho?
5. Who confessed his own sin and Israel's after seeing a vision of God on his throne?
6. What king confessed his adulterous affair after being confronted by the prophet Nathan?
7. What scribe bowed in front of the temple and confessed the sins of Israel while the people around him wept bitterly?
8. What young man confessed his riotous living to his forgiving father?
9. Who confessed the building of the golden calf to God?

6. Christ
7. Samuel (1 Samuel 9:16)
8. Zadok (1 Kings 1:39)
9. Jesus (Matthew 3:16)
10. Cyrus (Isaiah 45:1)
11. Messiah
12. Paul (2 Corinthians 1:21)
13. Moses (Exodus 40:9)
14. Samuel (1 Samuel 16:12)
15. Lucifer (Ezekiel 28:14—some translations have "the king of Tyre," not Lucifer)
16. Hebron (2 Samuel 2:4)

✦Healthy Confessions (Answers)

1. Manasseh (2 Chronicles 33:11-13)
2. David (2 Samuel 24:10)
3. Peter (Matthew 26:75)
4. Achan (Joshua 7:20)
5. Isaiah (6:5)
6. David (2 Samuel 12:13)
7. Ezra (10:1)
8. The prodigal son (Luke 15:18)
9. Moses (Exodus 32:31)

10. Who confessed his sexual immorality with his daughter-in-law, Tamar?
11. Who made a false confession to Aaron and Moses?
12. Who confessed his remorse over betraying his master?
13. Who confessed Israel's sins after he heard the walls of Jerusalem were in ruins?
14. Who was visited by the angel Gabriel while he was confessing his sins?
15. Who confessed that he had been self-righteous?
16. Who confessed his sin to an angel that only his donkey had seen?
17. Who was pardoned by David after confessing his sin and begging for mercy?
18. Who confessed to Samuel that he had disobeyed God by not destroying all the spoils of war?

◆Curses, Curses

1. What was the only animal to be cursed by God?
2. Who was sent by the king of Moab to put a curse on Israel?
3. What grandson of Noah was cursed for his father's sins?
4. Who cursed a fig tree for not bearing fruit?
5. Who put a curse on Cain and made him a wanderer?
6. What son of Josiah was cursed by God?
7. In what story did Jesus place a curse on the unrighteous?
8. According to Paul, what was put under a curse because of man's sin?
9. What nation did God say would have its towns and fields cursed because of disobedience?
10. What happened to the ground as a result of God's curse?
11. Who received a promise from God that all persons who cursed him would be cursed themselves?

10. Judah (Genesis 38:26)
11. Pharaoh (Exodus 10:16)
12. Judas (Matthew 27:4)
13. Nehemiah (1:6)
14. Daniel (9:20)
15. Job (42:6)
16. Balaam (Numbers 22:34)
17. Shimei (2 Samuel 19:20)
18. Saul (1 Samuel 15:24)

◆Curses, Curses (Answers)

1. The serpent (Genesis 3:14-15)
2. Balaam (Numbers 22:1-6)
3. Canaan (Genesis 4:11)
4. Jesus (Mark 11:21)
5. God (Genesis 4:11)
6. Jehoiakim (Jeremiah 22:18; 36:30)
7. The story of the sheep and the goats (Matthew 25:31-41)
8. Nature (Romans 8:19-22)
9. Israel (Deuteronomy 28:15-16)
10. It brought forth thorns and weeds (Genesis 3:17-18)
11. Abraham (Genesis 12:3)

12. According to Galatians, what people remain under a curse?
13. Who said that people who taught a false gospel would be cursed?
14. According to Paul, who was made a curse for our sins?
15. According to the Law, what sort of handicapped people should we not curse?
16. Who was told by his wife to curse God and die?
17. What prophet ended his book with God's threat to come and strike the land with a curse?
18. What epistle says that blessing and cursing should not come out of the same mouth?
19. Who had enemies that bound themselves under a curse because they were so determined to kill him?
20. Who told God that Job would curse him to his face?
21. What book says that kings should not be cursed, for little birds will tell on the cursing person?

12. Those who attempt to remain under the Law (Galatians 3:10)
13. Paul (Galatians 1:8)
14. Christ (Galatians 3:13)
15. The blind and the deaf (Leviticus 19:14)
16. Job (2:9)
17. Malachi (4:6)
18. James (3:10)
19. Paul (Acts 23:12)
20. Satan (Job 1:11; 2:5)
21. Ecclesiastes (10:20)

PART 5
Quote, Unquote

◆Who Said That? (I)

1. I have need to be baptized of thee, and comest thou to me?
2. I will not let thee go, except thou bless me.
3. We are all one man's sons; we are true men; thy servants are no spies.
4. Why, what evil hath he done? I have found no cause of death in him; I will therefore chastise him and let him go.
5. Let the day perish wherein I was born, and the night in which it was said, There is a man child conceived.
6. I go the way of all the earth; be thou strong therefore and show thyself a man.
7. Speak, for thy servant heareth.
8. Hath the Lord indeed spoken only by Moses? Hath he not spoken also by us?
9. I saw a dream which made me afraid, and the thoughts upon my bed and the visions of my head troubled me.
10. Let there be fair young virgins sought for the king.
11. Ye men of Athens, I perceive that in all things ye are too superstitious.
12. Behold, Lord, the half of my goods I give to the poor.
13. Set thine house in order; for thou shalt die, and not live.
14. Cursed be Canaan; a servant of servants shall he be unto his brethren.
15. Who am I, that I should go unto Pharaoh?

◆Who Said That? (I) (Answers)

1. John the Baptist (Matthew 3:14)
2. Jacob (Genesis 32:26)
3. Joseph's brothers (Genesis 42:11)
4. Pilate (Luke 23:22)
5. Job (3:3)
6. David (1 Kings 2:2)
7. Samuel (1 Samuel 3:10)
8. Miriam and Aaron (Numbers 12:2)
9. Nebuchadnezzar (Daniel 4:5)
10. Ahasuerus's servants (Esther 2:2)
11. Paul (Acts 17:22)
12. Zacchaeus (Luke 19:8)
13. Isaiah (2 Kings 20:1)
14. Noah (Genesis 9:25)
15. Moses (Exodus 3:11)

16. Remember the word which Moses the servant of the Lord commanded you, saying, The Lord your God hath given you rest, and hath given you this land.

17. I am but a little child; I know not how to go out or come in.

18. Oh, that my grief were thoroughly weighed, and my calamity laid in the balances together!

19. Ah, Lord God! Behold, I cannot speak, for I am a child.

20. This is John the Baptist; he is risen from the dead; and therefore mighty works do show forth themselves in him.

21. Ananias, why hath Satan filled thine heart to lie to the Holy Ghost, and to keep back part of the price of the land?

22. As many as I love, I rebuke and chasten; be zealous therefore, and repent.

23. Who is the Lord, that I should obey his voice to let Israel go?

24. Praise ye the Lord for the avenging of Israel, when the people willingly offered themselves.

25. Treason, treason.

26. What peace, so long as the whoredoms of thy mother Jezebel and her witchcrafts are so many?

27. O my son Absalom, O Absalom, my son, my son!

28. Woe is me, for I am undone!

29. I was no prophet, neither was I a prophet's son; but I was a herdsman, and a gatherer of sycamore fruit.

30. Depart from me; for I am a sinful man, O Lord.

31. Rabbi, we know that thou art a teacher come from God; for no man can do these miracles that thou doest, except God be with him.

32. Fear not, Mary; for thou hast found favor with God.

33. Ye stiffnecked and uncircumcised in heart and ears, ye do always resist the Holy Ghost.

34. I pray thee, of whom speaketh the prophet this? Of himself, or of some other man?

16. Joshua (1:13)
17. Solomon (1 Kings 3:7)
18. Job (6:2)
19. Jeremiah (1:6)
20. Herod (Matthew 14:2)
21. Peter (Acts 5:3)
22. Jesus (Revelation 3:19)
23. Pharaoh (Exodus 5:2)
24. Deborah and Barak (Judges 5:2)
25. Athaliah (2 Kings 11:14)
26. Jehu (2 Kings 9:22)
27. David (2 Samuel 19:4)
28. Isaiah (6:5)
29. Amos (7:14)
30. Peter (Luke 5:8)
31. Nicodemus (John 3:2)
32. Gabriel (Luke 1:30)
33. Stephen (Acts 7:51)
34. The Ethiopian eunuch (Acts 8:34)

35. Behold, thou hast mocked me, and told me lies; now
    tell me, I pray thee, wherewith thou mightest be
    bound.
36. Why are ye come out to set your battle in array? Am
    I not a Philistine, and ye servants to Saul?
37. I have found the book of the law in the house of the
    Lord.
38. Skin for skin, yea, all that a man hath will he give for
    his life.
39. Thou, O king, art a king of kings; for the God of
    heaven hath given thee a kingdom, power, and
    strength, and glory.
40. Where is he that is born King of the Jews?
41. Why should it be thought a thing incredible with you,
    that God should raise the dead?
42. The Lord is my rock, and my fortress, and my
    deliverer.
43. If I be a man of God, let fire come down from
    heaven, and consume thee and thy fifty.
44. Dost thou still retain thine integrity? Curse God and
    die.
45. It was a true report that I heard in mine own land of
    thy acts and of thy wisdom.
46. Why is thy countenance sad, seeing thou art not
    sick? This is nothing else but sorrow of heart.
47. O thou seer, go, flee thee away to Judah, and there
    eat bread, and prophesy there, but prophesy not
    again any more at Bethel.
48. Master, we saw one casting out devils in thy name,
    and he followeth not us; and we forbade him,
    because he followeth not us.
49. Why was not this ointment sold for three hundred
    pence, and given to the poor?
50. What shall I do unto this people? They be almost
    ready to stone me.
51. The scepter shall not depart from Judah, nor a
    lawgiver from between his feet, until Shiloh come.
52. The serpent beguiled me, and I did eat.

35. Delilah (Judges 16:10)
36. Goliath (1 Samuel 17:8)
37. Hilkiah (2 Kings 22:8)
38. Satan (Job 2:4)
39. Daniel (2:37)
40. The wise men (Matthew 2:2)
41. Paul (Acts 26:8)
42. David (2 Samuel 22:2)
43. Elijah (2 Kings 1:10)
44. Job's wife (Job 2:9)
45. The queen of Sheba (1 Kings 10:6)
46. Artaxerxes (Nehemiah 2:2)
47. Amaziah (Amos 7:12-13)
48. John (Mark 9:38)
49. Judas Iscariot (John 12:5)
50. Moses (Exodus 17:4)
51. Jacob (Genesis 49:10)
52. Eve (Genesis 3:13)

53. Turn again, my daughters. Why will ye go with me? Are there yet any more sons in my womb, that they may be your husbands?

54. Had Zimri peace, who slew his master?

55. Take heed now; for the Lord hath chosen thee to build a house for the sanctuary; be strong, and do it.

56. Behold, a virgin shall conceive, and bear a son, and shall call his name Immanuel.

57. I heard thy voice in the garden, and I was afraid.

58. Get thee from me, take heed to thyself, see my face no more; for in that day thou seest my face thou shalt die.

59. My punishment is greater than I can bear.

60. How long halt ye between two opinions? If the Lord be God, follow him; but if Baal, then follow him.

61. Out of the eater came forth meat, and out of the strong came forth sweetness.

62. He will take your daughters to be confectionaries, and to be cooks, and to be bakers.

63. What hast thou to do with peace? Turn thee behind me.

64. He must increase, but I must decrease.

65. Therefore let all the house of Israel know assuredly, that God hath made that same Jesus, whom ye have crucified, both Lord and Christ.

66. Lord God, what wilt thou give me, seeing I go childless, and the steward of my house is this Eliezer of Damascus?

67. Shall I go and call to thee a nurse of the Hebrew women, that she may nurse the child for thee?

68. What have I done unto thee, that thou hast smitten me these three times?

69. Master, behold, the fig tree which thou cursedst is withered away.

70. Repent and be baptized every one of you in the name of Jesus Christ for the remission of sins.

71. Behold, I see the heavens opened, and the Son of man standing on the right hand of God.

53. Naomi (Ruth 1:11)
54. Jezebel (2 Kings 9:31)
55. David (1 Chronicles 28:10)
56. Isaiah (7:14)
57. Adam (Genesis 3:10)
58. Pharaoh (Exodus 10:28)
59. Cain (Genesis 4:13)
60. Elijah (1 Kings 18:21)
61. Samson (Judges 14:14)
62. Samuel (1 Samuel 8:13)
63. Jehu (2 Kings 9:19)
64. John the Baptist (John 3:30)
65. Peter (Acts 2:36)
66. Abraham (Genesis 15:2)
67. Miriam (Exodus 2:7)
68. Balaam's donkey (Numbers 22:28)
69. Peter (Mark 11:21)
70. Peter (Acts 2:38)
71. Stephen (Acts 7:56)

72. What shall be the sign that the Lord will heal me, and that I shall go up into the house of the Lord the third day?

73. Lord God of Abraham, Isaac, and Israel, let it be known this day that thou art God in Israel.

74. Behold now, the Lord hath restrained me from bearing. I pray thee, go in unto my maid; it may be that I may obtain children by her.

75. There shall come a star out of Jacob, and a scepter shall rise out of Israel.

76. Let me die with the Philistines.

77. Let not my lord, I pray thee, regard this man of Belial, even Nabal; for as his name is, so is he; Nabal is his name, and folly is with him.

78. My father made your yoke heavy, and I will add to your yoke.

79. After I am waxed old, shall I have pleasure, my lord being old also?

80. I know that the Lord hath given you the land, and that your terror is fallen upon us, and that all the inhabitants of the land faint because of you.

81. Can the blind lead the blind? Shall they not both fall into the ditch?

82. Cast out this bondwoman and her son; for the son of this bondwoman shall not be heir with my son.

83. Entreat me not to leave thee, or to return from following after thee; for whither thou goest, I will go.

84. My father chastised you with whips, but I will chastise you with scorpions.

85. I know thou canst do everything, and that no thought can be withholden from thee.

86. If it seems good unto the king, let the king and Haman come this day unto the banquet that I have prepared for him.

87. Behold the handmaid of the Lord.

88. Of a truth I perceive that God is no respecter of persons.

89. It is hard for thee to kick against the pricks.

72. Hezekiah (2 Kings 20:8)
73. Elijah (1 Kings 18:36)
74. Sarah (Genesis 16:2)
75. Balaam (Numbers 24:17)
76. Samson (Judges 16:30)
77. Abigail (1 Samuel 25:25)
78. Rehoboam (1 Kings 12:14)
79. Sarah (Genesis 18:12)
80. Rahab (Joshua 2:9)
81. Jesus (Luke 6:39)
82. Sarah (Genesis 21:10)
83. Ruth (1:16)
84. Rehoboam (1 Kings 12:14)
85. Job (42:2)
86. Esther (5:4)
87. Mary (Luke 1:38)
88. Peter (Acts 10:34)
89. Jesus (Acts 9:5)

90. This is one of the Hebrews' children.
91. Saul hath slain his thousands, and David his ten thousands.
92. Am I a dog, that thou comest to me with staves?
93. Behold, the days come, that all that is in thine house, and that which thy fathers have laid up in store unto this day, shall be carried into Babylon.
94. Wilt thou also destroy the righteous with the wicked?
95. I find no fault in this man.

✦What Gets Quoted Most?

1. What book, one of the prophets, gets quoted in the New Testament more than any Old Testament book (419 times)?
2. What book, the longest in the Old Testament, ranks second with 414 references in the New?
3. What book, part of the Torah, ranks third with 260 references?
4. What book, part narrative and part law, ranks fourth with 250 references?
5. What book, more law than history, ranks fifth with 208 references?
6. What book, a long book of prophecy, ranks sixth with 141 references?
7. What book, with many visions in it, ranks seventh with 133 references?
8. What book, a book by one of the later prophets, ranks eighth with 125 references?
9. What book, probably one of the least read of Old Testament books, ranks ninth with 107 references?
10. What book, mostly history and part law, ranks tenth with 73 references?

90. Pharaoh's daughter (Exodus 2:6)
91. The women of Israel (1 Samuel 18:7)
92. Goliath (1 Samuel 17:43)
93. Isaiah (2 Kings 20:17)
94. Abraham (Genesis 18:23)
95. Pilate (Luke 23:4)

✦What Gets Quoted Most? (Answers)

1. Isaiah
2. Psalms
3. Genesis
4. Exodus
5. Deuteronomy
6. Ezekiel
7. Daniel
8. Jeremiah
9. Leviticus
10. Numbers

✦Everyday Phrases from the Bible

Identify the book and, if possible, the chapter and verse where these commonly used phrases originated.

1. The skin of my teeth.
2. Wolf in sheep's clothing.
3. Salt of the earth.
4. Holier than thou.
5. Woe is me!
6. Can a leopard change his spots?
7. A drop in a bucket.
8. Eat, drink, and be merry.
9. Pride goeth before a fall.
10. Give up the ghost.
11. Spare the rod and spoil the child.
12. My brother's keeper.
13. Fat of the land.
14. A lamb for the slaughter.
15. The blind leading the blind.

✦The Old Testament in the New (I)

Each of these passages from the New Testament is a quotation from the Old Testament. Name the Old Testament book (and, if you're sharp, chapter and verse) where the passage appears.

1. "Behold, a virgin shall be with child, and shall bring forth a son, and they shall call his name Emmanuel" (Matthew 1:23).
2. "Prepare ye the way of the Lord, make his paths straight" (Matthew 3:3).
3. "The people which sat in darkness saw great light; and to them which sat in the region and shadow of death light is sprung up" (Matthew 4:16).

✦Everyday Phrases from the Bible (Answers)

1. "I am escaped with the skin of my teeth" (Job 19:20)
2. "Beware of false prophets, which come to you in sheep's clothing, but inwardly they are ravening wolves" (Matthew 7:15)
3. "Ye are the salt of the earth" (Matthew 5:13)
4. "I am holier than thou" (Isaiah 65:5)
5. "Woe is me! for I am undone" (Isaiah 6:5)
6. "Can the Ethiopian change his skin, or the leopard his spots?" (Jeremiah 13:23)
7. "Behold, the nations are as a drop of a bucket, and are counted as the small dust of the balance" (Isaiah 40:15)
8. "A man hath no better thing under the sun, than to eat, and to drink and to be merry" (Ecclesiastes 8:15)
9. "Pride goeth before destruction, and an haughty spirit before a fall" (Proverbs 16:18)
10. "But man dieth, and wasteth away; yea, man giveth up the ghost, and where is he?" (Job 14:10)
11. "He that spareth the rod hateth his son" (Proverbs 13:24)
12. "Am I my brother's keeper?" (Genesis 4:9)
13. "And he shall eat the fat of the land" (Genesis 45:18)
14. "He is brought as a lamb to the slaughter" (Isaiah 53:7)
15. "If a blind man leads a blind man, both will fall into a pit" (Matthew 15:14)

✦The Old Testament in the New (I) (Answers)

1. Isaiah 7:14
2. Isaiah 40:3
3. Isaiah 42:7

4. "Man shall not live by bread alone, but by every word that proceedeth out of the mouth of God" (Matthew 4:4).

5. "Thou shalt not tempt the Lord thy God" (Matthew 4:7).

6. "Thou shalt worship the Lord thy God, and him only shalt thou serve" (Matthew 4:10).

7. "An eye for an eye, and a tooth for a tooth" (Matthew 5:38).

8. "Thou shalt love thy neighbor, and hate thine enemy" (Matthew 5:43).

9. "Himself took our iniquities, and bare our sicknesses" (Matthew 8:17).

10. "I will have mercy, and not sacrifice" (Matthew 9:13).

11. "Behold, I send my messenger before my face, which shall prepare thy way before thee" (Matthew 11:10).

12. "Behold my servant, whom I have chosen; my beloved, in whom my soul is well pleased; I will put my spirit upon him, and he shall show judgment to the Gentiles" (Matthew 12:18).

13. "He shall not strive, nor cry; neither shall any man hear his voice in the streets" (Matthew 12:19).

14. "A bruised reed shall he not break, and smoking flax shall he not quench, till he send forth judgment unto victory" (Matthew 12:20).

15. "And in his name shall the Gentiles trust" (Matthew 12:21).

16. "By hearing ye shall hear, and shall not understand; and seeing ye shall see, and shall not perceive" (Matthew 13:14).

17. "For this people's heart is waxed gross, and their ears are dull of hearing, and their eyes they have closed" (Matthew 13:15).

18. "I will open my mouth in parables; I will utter things which have been kept secret from the foundation of the world" (Matthew 13:35).

4. Deuteronomy 8:3
5. Deuteronomy 6:16
6. Deuteronomy 6:13
7. Exodus 21:24
8. Leviticus 19:18
9. Isaiah 53:4
10. Hosea 6:6
11. Malachi 3:1
12. Isaiah 42:1
13. Isaiah 42:2
14. Isaiah 42:3
15. Isaiah 42:4
16. Isaiah 6:9
17. Isaiah 6:10
18. Psalm 78:2

19. "This people draweth nigh unto me with their mouth, and honoreth me with their lips; but their heart is far from me" (Matthew 15:8).

20. "My house shall be a house of prayer" (Matthew 21:13).

21. "Out of the mouth of babes and sucklings thou hast perfected praise" (Matthew 21:16).

22. "The stone which the builders rejected, the same is become the head of the corner" (Matthew 21:42).

23. "I am the God of Abraham, and the God of Isaac, and the God of Jacob" (Matthew 22:32).

24. "Thou shalt love the Lord thy God with all thy heart, and with all thy soul, and with all thy mind" (Matthew 22:37).

25. "Thou shalt love thy neighbor as thyself" (Matthew 22:39).

26. "The Lord said unto my Lord, Sit thou on my right hand, till I make thine enemies thy footstool" (Matthew 22:44).

27. "They parted my garments among them, and upon my vesture did they cast lots" (Matthew 27:35).

28. "He trusted in God; let him deliver him now" (Matthew 27:43).

29. "My God, my God, why hast thou forsaken me?" (Matthew 27:46).

30. "The voice of one crying in the wilderness, Prepare ye the way of the Lord" (Mark 1:3).

31. "That seeing they may see, and not perceive; and hearing they may hear, and not understand; lest at any time they should be converted, and their sins should be forgiven them" (Mark 4:12).

32. "This people honoreth me with their lips, but their heart is far from me" (Mark 7:6).

33. "For this cause shall a man leave his father and mother, and cleave to his wife; and they twain shall be one flesh" (Mark 10:7-8).

34. "Where their worm dieth not, and the fire is not quenched" (Mark 9:48).

19. Isaiah 29:13
20. Isaiah 56:7
21. Psalm 8:2
22. Psalm 118:22
23. Exodus 3:6
24. Deuteronomy 6:3
25. Leviticus 19:18
26. Psalm 110:1
27. Psalm 22:18
28. Psalm 22:8
29. Psalm 22:1
30. Isaiah 40:3
31. Isaiah 6:9
32. Isaiah 29:13
33. Genesis 2:24
34. Isaiah 66:24

35. "For everyone shall be salted with fire, and every sacrifice shall be salted with salt" (Mark 9:49).
36. "Hear, O Israel; The Lord our God is one Lord" (Mark 12:29).
37. "I will smite the shepherd, and the sheep shall be scattered" (Mark 14:27).
38. "Every male that openeth the womb shall be called holy to the Lord" (Luke 2:23).
39. "Every valley shall be filled, and every mountain and hill shall be brought low" (Luke 3:5).
40. "And all flesh shall see the salvation of God" (Luke 3:6).
41. "He shall give his angels charge over thee, to keep thee" (Luke 4:10).
42. "They shall bear thee up, lest at any time thou dash thy foot against a stone" (Luke 4:11).
43. "The Spirit of the Lord is upon me, because he hath anointed me to preach the gospel to the poor" (Luke 4:18).
44. "That seeing they might not see, and hearing they might not understand" (Luke 8:10).
45. "My house is the house of prayer" (Luke 19:46).
46. "Make straight the way of the Lord" (John 1:23).
47. "The zeal of thine house hath eaten me up" (John 2:17).
48. "Ye are gods" (John 10:34).
49. "Behold, thy king cometh, sitting on an ass's colt" (John 12:15).
50. "Lord, who hath believed our report? and to whom hath the arm of the Lord been revealed?" (John 12:38).
51. "He hath blinded their eyes, and hardened their heart" (John 12:40).
52. "He that eateth bread with me hath lifted up his heel against me" (John 13:18).
53. "They hated me without a cause" (John 15:25).
54. "They shall look on him whom they pierced" (John 19:37).

35. Leviticus 2:13
36. Deuteronomy 6:4
37. Zechariah 13:7
38. Exodus 13:2
39. Isaiah 40:3-4
40. Isaiah 40:5
41. Psalm 91:11
42. Psalm 91:12
43. Isaiah 61:1
44. Isaiah 6:9
45. Isaiah 56:7
46. Isaiah 40:3
47. Psalm 69:9
48. Psalm 82:6
49. Zechariah 9:9
50. Isaiah 53:1
51. Isaiah 6:9
52. Psalm 41:9
53. Psalm 35:19
54. Zechariah 12:10

55. "A bone of him shall not be broken" (John 19:36).
56. "Let his habitation be desolate, and let no man dwell therein" (Acts 1:20).
57. "And it shall come to pass in the last days, saith God, I will pour out my Spirit upon all flesh; and your sons and daughters shall prophesy, and your young men shall see visions, and your old men shall dream dreams" (Acts 2:17).
58. "The sun shall be turned into darkness, and the moon into blood, before that great and notable day of the Lord come" (Acts 2:20).
59. "I foresaw the Lord always before my face, for he is on my right hand, that I should not be moved" (Acts 2:25).
60. "Thou wilt not leave my soul in hell, neither wilt thou suffer thine Holy One to see corruption" (Acts 2:27).
61. "The Lord said to my Lord, Sit thou on my right hand" (Acts 2:34).
62. "A prophet shall the Lord your God raise up unto you of your brethren, like unto me; him shall ye hear in all things whatsoever he shall say unto you" (Acts 3:22).
63. "This is the stone which was set at nought by you builders, which is become the head of the corner" (Acts 4:11).
64. "Why did the heathen rage, and the people imagine vain things?" (Acts 4:25).
65. "Put off thy shoes from thy feet: for the place where thou standest is holy ground" (Acts 7:33).
66. "I have seen the affliction of my people which is in Egypt, and I have heard their groaning, and am come down to deliver them" (Acts 7:34).
67. "Make us gods to go before us; for as for this Moses, which brought us out of the land of Egypt, we wot not what is become of him" (Acts 7:40).

55. Exodus 12:46
56. Psalm 69:25
57. Joel 2:28
58. Joel 2:31
59. Psalm 16:8
60. Psalm 16:10
61. Psalm 110:1
62. Deuteronomy 18:15
63. Psalm 118:22
64. Psalm 2:1
65. Exodus 3:5
66. Exodus 3:7
67. Exodus 32:1

68. "O ye house of Israel, have ye offered to me slain beasts and sacrifices by the space of forty years in the wilderness?" (Acts 7:42).
69. "He was led as a sheep to the slaughter: and like a lamb dumb before a shearer, so opened he not his mouth" (Acts 8:32).
70. "In his humiliation his judgment was taken away: and who shall declare his generation? For his life is taken from the earth" (Acts 8:33).

✦Who Said That? (II)

1. Lord, lay not this sin to their charge.
2. See, here is water; what doth hinder me to be baptized?
3. I die, and God will surely visit you, and bring you out of this land unto the land which he sware to Abraham, to Isaac, and to Jacob.
4. Thou art Peter, and upon this rock I will build my church.
5. Behold, this child is set for the fall and rising again of many in Israel.
6. And put my cup, the silver cup, in the sack's mouth of the youngest, and his corn money.
7. Now shall I be more blameless than the Philistines, though I do them a displeasure.
8. I am a Hebrew, and I fear the Lord, the God of heaven, which hath made the sea and the dry land.
9. There cometh one mightier than I after me, the latchet of whose shoes I am not worthy to stoop down and unloose.
10. The God of our fathers raised up Jesus, whom ye slew and hanged on a tree.
11. As the Lord liveth, the man that hath done this thing shall surely die.

68. Amos 5:25
69. Isaiah 53:7
70. Isaiah 53:8

✦Who Said That? (II) (Answers)

1. Stephen (Acts 7:60)
2. The Ethiopian eunuch (Acts 8:36)
3. Joseph (Genesis 50:24)
4. Jesus (Matthew 16:18)
5. Simeon (Luke 2:34)
6. Joseph (Genesis 44:2)
7. Samson (Judges 15:3)
8. Jonah (1:9)
9. John the Baptist (Mark 1:7)
10. Peter (Acts 5:30)
11. David (2 Samuel 12:5)

12. Draw thy sword, and thrust me through therewith, lest these uncircumcised come and thrust me through, and abuse me.
13. Lie with me.
14. I have sinned this time; the Lord is righteous, and I and my people are wicked.
15. Give me thy vineyard, that I may have it for a garden of herbs, because it is near my house; and I will give thee for it a better vineyard.
16. Behold, I have given Esther the house of Haman, and him they have hanged upon the gallows, because he laid his hand upon the Jews.
17. Whoever shall read this writing, and show me the interpretation thereof, shall be clothed with scarlet, and have a chain of gold about his neck, and shall be the third ruler in the kingdom.
18. My soul doth magnify the Lord.
19. All these things will I give thee, if thou wilt fall down and worship me.
20. Repent ye; for the kingdom of heaven is at hand.
21. Men and brethren, I am a Pharisee, the son of a Pharisee; of the hope and resurrection of the dead I am called into question.
22. Silver and gold have I none; but such as I have I give thee: In the name of Jesus Christ of Nazareth, rise up and walk.
23. The voice is Jacob's voice, but the hands are the hands of Esau.
24. How are the mighty fallen, and the weapons of war perished!
25. If now I have found grace in thy sight, then show me a sign that thou talkest with me.
26. Ye have brought this man unto me, as one that perverteth the people; and behold, I, having examined him before you, have found no fault in this man touching those things whereof ye accuse him.

12. Saul (1 Samuel 31:4)
13. Potiphar's wife (Genesis 39:7)
14. Pharaoh (Exodus 9:27)
15. Ahab (1 Kings 21:2)
16. Ahasuerus (Esther 8:7)
17. Belshazzar (Daniel 5:7)
18. Mary (Luke 1:46)
19. The devil (Matthew 4:9)
20. John the Baptist (Matthew 3:2)
21. Paul (Acts 23:6)
22. Peter (Acts 3:6)
23. Isaac (Genesis 27:22)
24. David (2 Samuel 1:27)
25. Gideon (Judges 6:17)
26. Pilate (Luke 23:14)

27. Dost thou now govern the kingdom of Israel? Arise, and eat bread, and let thine heart be merry. I will give thee the vineyard of Naboth.
28. Of a truth it is, that your God is a God of gods, and a Lord of kings, and a revealer of secrets, seeing thou couldest reveal this secret.
29. These things have I spoken unto you, that in me ye might have peace.
30. He hath brought in a Hebrew to mock us; he came in unto me to lie with me, and I cried with a loud voice.
31. Entreat the Lord, that he may take away the frogs from me and from my people.
32. Hearest thou not, my daughter? Go not to glean in another field, neither go from hence, but abide here fast by my maidens.
33. But will God indeed dwell on the earth? Behold, the heaven and heaven of heavens cannot contain thee; how much less this house that I have builded?
34. Have thou nothing to do with that just man; for I have suffered many things this day in a dream because of him.
35. I am he that liveth, and was dead; and behold, I am alive for evermore.
36. Thou art the man.
37. Behold, to obey is better than sacrifice, and to hearken than the fat of rams.
38. I have been a Nazarite unto God from my mother's womb; if I be shaven, then my strength will go from me.
39. I have heard many such things; miserable comforters are ye all.
40. No, my lord, I am a woman of sorrowful spirit; I have drunk neither wine nor strong drink, but have poured out my soul before the Lord.
41. Thy brother came with subtilty, and hath taken away thy blessing.
42. Men and brethren, I have lived in all good conscience before until this day.

27. Jezebel (1 Kings 21:7)
28. Nebuchadnezzar (Daniel 2:47)
29. Jesus (John 16:33)
30. Potiphar's wife (Genesis 39:14)
31. Pharaoh (Exodus 8:8)
32. Boaz (Ruth 2:8)
33. Solomon (1 Kings 8:27)
34. Pilate's wife (Matthew 27:19)
35. Jesus (Revelation 1:18)
36. Nathan (2 Samuel 12:7)
37. Samuel (1 Samuel 15:22)
38. Samson (Judges 16:17)
39. Job (16:2)
40. Hannah (1 Samuel 1:15)
41. Isaac (Genesis 27:35)
42. Paul (Acts 23:1)

43. Will ye that I release unto you the King of the Jews?
44. Yet forty days and Nineveh shall be overthrown.
45. Certainly this was a righteous man.
46. My Lord and my God.
47. Thy people shall be my people, and thy God my God.
48. The Philistines be upon thee, Samson.
49. Go ye, serve the Lord; only let your flocks and your herds be stayed; let your little ones also go with you.
50. The Lord watch between me and thee, when we are absent one from another.
51. O Lord, take, I beseech thee, my life from me; for it is better for me to die than to live.
52. Go and search diligently for the young child; and when ye have found him, bring me word again, that I may come and worship him also.
53. The Lord forbid that I should stretch forth mine hand against the Lord's anointed.
54. Naked came I out of my mother's womb, and naked shall I return thither. The Lord gave, and the Lord hath taken away; blessed be the name of the Lord.
55. Here am I, send me.
56. Prove thy servants, I beseech thee, ten days; and let them give us pulse to eat, and water to drink.
57. We have a father, an old man, and a child of his old age, a little one.
58. Am I my brother's keeper?
59. God that made the world and all things therein, seeing that he is Lord of heaven and earth, dwelleth not in temples made with hands.
60. Lord, it is good for us to be here; if thou wilt, let us make here three tabernacles; one for thee, and one for Moses, and one for Elias.
61. Refrain from these men, and let them alone; for if this counsel or this work be of men, it will come to nought.

43. Pilate (Mark 15:9)
44. Jonah (3:4)
45. The centurion at the Crucifixion (Luke 23:47)
46. Thomas (John 20:28)
47. Ruth (1:16)
48. Delilah (Judges 16:20)
49. Pharaoh (Exodus 10:24)
50. Laban (Genesis 31:49)
51. Jonah (4:3)
52. Herod (Matthew 2:8)
53. David (1 Samuel 26:11)
54. Job (1:21)
55. Isaiah (6:8)
56. Daniel (1:12)
57. Judah (Genesis 44:20)
58. Cain (Genesis 4:9)
59. Paul (Acts 17:24)
60. Peter (Matthew 17:4)
61. Gamaliel (Acts 5:38)

62. Lord, now lettest thou thy servant depart in peace, according to thy word; for mine eyes have seen thy salvation.

63. Blessed be the God of Shadrach, Meshach, and Abednego, who hath sent his angel, and delivered his servants that trusted in him.

64. This day is this scripture fulfilled in your ears.

65. Almost thou persuadest me to be a Christian.

66. Now therefore are we all here present before God, to hear all things that are commanded thee of God.

67. Behold, the people of the children of Israel are more and mightier than we.

68. Shall a child be born unto him that is an hundred years old?

69. This will be the manner of the king that shall reign over you: He will take your sons, and appoint them for himself, for his chariots, and to be his horsemen.

70. Give therefore thy servant an understanding heart to judge thy people, that I may discern between good and bad; for who is able to judge this thy so great a people?

71. There is a certain people scattered abroad and dispersed among the people in all the provinces of thy kingdom; and their laws are diverse from all people; neither keep they the king's laws.

72. For before the child shall know to refuse the evil, and choose the good, the land that thou abhorrest shall be forsaken of both her kings.

73. Full well ye reject the commandment of God, that ye may keep your own tradition.

74. Great is Diana of the Ephesians.

75. What is truth?

76. Can there be any good thing come out of Nazareth?

77. Cry aloud, for he is a god; either he is talking, or he is pursuing, or he is in a journey, or peradventure he sleepeth, and must be awaked.

62. Simeon (Luke 2:29-30)
63. Nebuchadnezzar (Daniel 3:28)
64. Jesus (Luke 4:21)
65. Agrippa (Acts 26:28)
66. Cornelius (Acts 10:33)
67. Pharaoh (Exodus 1:9)
68. Abraham (Genesis 17:17)
69. Samuel (1 Samuel 8:11)
70. Solomon (1 Kings 3:9)
71. Haman (Esther 3:8)
72. Isaiah (7:16)
73. Jesus (Mark 7:9)
74. The people of Ephesus (Acts 19:34)
75. Pilate (John 18:38)
76. Nathanael (John 1:46)
77. Elijah (1 Kings 18:27)

78. Let me, I pray thee, kiss my father and my mother, and then I will follow thee.
79. In what place soever ye enter into an house, there abide till ye depart from that place.
80. How can a man be born when he is old? Can he enter the second time into his mother's womb, and be born?
81. Go, see now this cursed woman, and bury her; for she is a king's daughter.
82. I have heard of thee by the hearing of the ear; but now mine eye seeth thee.
83. God Almighty appeared unto me at Luz in the land of Canaan, and blessed me.
84. The woman whom thou gavest to be with me, she gave me of the tree, and I did eat.
85. Is it true, O Shadrach, Meshach, and Abednego, do not ye serve my gods, nor worship the golden image which I have set up?
86. Not so, Lord, for I have never eaten anything that is common or unclean.
87. He hath regarded the low estate of his handmaiden; for, behold, from henceforth all generations shall call me blessed.
88. Is it not because the Lord hath anointed thee to be captain over his inheritance?
89. And now, my daughter, fear not; I will do to thee all that thou requirest; for all the city of my people doth know that thou art a virtuous woman.
90. Ye men of Judea, and all ye that dwell at Jerusalem, be this known unto you, and hearken to my words; for these are not drunken, as ye suppose, seeing it is but the third hour of the day.
91. Thus saith the king, Let not Hezekiah deceive you; for he shall not be able to deliver you out of his hand.
92. Give me here John the Baptist's head in a charger.
93. Truth, Lord, yet the dogs eat of the crumbs which fall from their master's table.

78. Elisha (1 Kings 19:20)
79. Jesus (Mark 6:10)
80. Nicodemus (John 3:4)
81. Jehu (2 Kings 9:34)
82. Job (42:5)
83. Jacob (Genesis 48:3)
84. Adam (Genesis 3:12)
85. Nebuchadnezzar (Daniel 3:14)
86. Peter (Acts 10:14)
87. Mary (Luke 1:48)
88. Samuel (1 Samuel 10:1)
89. Boaz (Ruth 3:11)
90. Peter (Acts 2:14-15)
91. Rabshakeh (2 Kings 18:29)
92. The daughter of Herodias (Matthew 14:8)
93. The Canaanite woman (Matthew 15:27)

94. What therefore God hath joined together, let not man put asunder.
95. Every man at the beginning doth set forth good wine; and when men have well drunk, then that which is worse; but thou hast kept the good wine until now.

✦Chapter 1, Verse 1

Each of the following is the first verse of a book of the Bible. Name the book in each case.

1. The beginning of the gospel of Jesus Christ, the Son of God.
2. Blessed is the man that walketh not in the counsel of the ungodly.
3. There was a man in the land of Uz.
4. The former treatise have I made, O Theophilus, of all that Jesus began to do and teach.
5. The elder unto the well-beloved Gaius, whom I love in the truth.
6. In the third year of the reign of Jehoiakim king of Judah came Nebuchadnezzar king of Babylon unto Jerusalem and besieged it.
7. Now these are the names of the children of Israel, which came unto Egypt; every man and his household came with Jacob.
8. The words of the Preacher, the son of David, king in Jerusalem.
9. God, who at sundry times and in divers manners spake in times past unto the fathers by the prophets.
10. That which was from the beginning, which we have heard, which we have seen with our eyes, which we have looked upon, and our hands have handled, of the Word of life.
11. And the Lord called unto Moses, and spake unto him out of the tabernacle of the congregation.
12. Adam, Sheth, Enosh.

94. Jesus (Mark 10:9)
95. The ruler of the marriage feast at Cana (John 2:10)

◆Chapter 1, Verse 1 (Answers)

1. Mark
2. Psalms
3. Job
4. Acts
5. 3 John
6. Daniel
7. Exodus
8. Ecclesiastes
9. Hebrews
10. 1 John
11. Leviticus
12. 1 Chronicles

13. The book of the generation of Jesus Christ, the son of David, the son of Abraham.

14. Paul, an apostle of Jesus Christ by the commandment of God our Savior, and Lord Jesus Christ, which is our hope.

15. Now it came to pass in the days of Ahasuerus (this is Ahasuerus which reigned, from India even unto Ethiopia, over an hundred and seven and twenty provinces).

16. How doth the city sit solitary, that was full of people! How is she become as a widow!

17. In the beginning was the Word, and the Word was with God, and the Word was God.

18. Now it came to pass in the thirtieth year, in the fourth month, in the fifth day of the month, as I was among the captives by the river of Chebar, that the heavens were opened, and I saw visions of God.

19. Paul, an apostle (not of men, neither by man, but by Jesus Christ, and God the father, who raised him from the dead).

20. In the beginning God created the heaven and the earth.

21. And the Lord spake unto Moses in the wilderness of Sinai, in the tabernacle of the congregation, on the first day of the second month, in the second year after they were come out of the land of Egypt.

22. And Solomon the son of David was strengthened in his kingdom, and the Lord his God was with him, and magnified him exceedingly.

23. The elder unto the elect lady and her children, whom I love in the truth; and not I only, but also all they that have known the truth.

24. Paul, a servant of Jesus Christ, called to be an apostle, separated unto the gospel of God.

25. Now there was a certain man of Ramathaim-zophim, of mount Ephraim, and his name was Elkanah, the son of Jeroham, the son of Elihu, the son of Tohu, the son of Zuph, an Ephrathite.

13. Matthew
14. 1 Timothy
15. Esther
16. Lamentations
17. John
18. Ezekiel
19. Galatians
20. Genesis
21. Numbers
22. 2 Chronicles
23. 2 John
24. Romans
25. 1 Samuel

26. Now in the first year of Cyrus king of Persia, that the word of the Lord by the mouth of Jeremiah might be fulfilled, the Lord stirred up the spirit of Cyrus king of Persia, that he made a proclamation throughout all his kingdom.

27. Then Moab rebelled against Israel after the death of Ahab.

28. These be the words which Moses spake unto all Israel on this side Jordan in the wilderness, in the plain over against the Red Sea, between Paran and Tophel and Laban and Hazeroth and Dizahab.

29. Paul, a servant of God, and an apostle of Jesus Christ, according to the faith of God's elect, and the acknowledging of the truth which is after godliness.

30. Now it came to pass after the death of Saul, when David was returned from the slaughter of the Amalekites, and David had abode two days in Ziklag.

31. Forasmuch as many have taken in hand to set forth in order a declaration of those things which are most surely believed among us.

32. Paul, called to be an apostle of Jesus Christ through the will of God, and Sosthenes our brother.

33. Now King David was old and stricken in years; and they covered him with clothes, but he got no heat.

34. Now after the death of Joshua it came to pass, that the children of Israel asked the Lord.

◆Beginning at the End

Each of the following is the last verse of a book of the Bible. Name the book in each case.

1. Remember me, O my God, for good.
2. But thou hast utterly rejected us; thou art very wroth against us.
3. And they were continually in the temple, praising and blessing God. Amen.

26. Ezra
27. 2 Kings
28. Deuteronomy
29. Titus
30. 2 Samuel
31. Luke
32. 1 Corinthians
33. 1 Kings
34. Judges

✦Beginning at the End (Answers)

1. Nehemiah
2. Lamentations
3. Luke

4. For he served Baal, and worshipped him, and provoked to anger the Lord God of Israel, according to all that his father had done.

5. And Eleazar the son of Aaron died; and they buried him in a hill that pertained to Phinehas his son, which was given him in Mount Ephraim.

6. And for his diet, there was a continual diet given him of the king of Babylon, every day a portion until the day of his death, all the days of his life.

7. The grace of our Lord Jesus Christ be with you all. Amen.

8. So Joseph died, being a hundred and ten years old; and they embalmed him, and he was put in a coffin in Egypt.

9. And David built there an altar unto the Lord, and offered burnt offerings and peace offerings. So the Lord was entreated for the land, and the plague was stayed from Israel.

10. Let every thing that hath breath praise the Lord. Praise ye the Lord.

11. For I will make you a name and a praise among all people of the earth, when I turn back your captivity before your eyes, saith the Lord.

12. For God shall bring every work into judgment, with every secret thing, whether it be good, or whether it be evil.

13. To God only wise, be glory through Jesus Christ forever. Amen.

14. For their worm shall not die, neither shall their fire be quenched; and they shall be an abhorring unto all flesh.

15. Give her of the fruit of her hands; and let her own words praise her in the gates.

16. The salutation by the hand of me Paul. Remember my bonds. Grace be with you. Amen.

17. But go thou thy way till the end be; for thou shalt rest, and stand in thy lot at the end of the days.

4. 1 Kings
5. Joshua
6. Jeremiah
7. Philippians, Revelation
8. Genesis
9. 2 Samuel
10. Psalms
11. Zephaniah
12. Ecclesiastes
13. Romans
14. Isaiah
15. Proverbs
16. Colossians
17. Daniel

18. But I trust I shall shortly see thee, and we shall speak face to face. Peace be to thee. Our friends salute thee. Greet the friends by name.

19. With all his reign and his might, and the times that went over him, and over Israel, and over all the kingdoms of the countries.

20. And they went out quickly, and fled from the sepulchre; for they trembled and were amazed; neither said they anything to any man, for they were afraid.

21. For the cloud of the Lord was upon the tabernacle by day, and fire was on it by night, in the sight of all the house of Israel, throughout all their journeys.

22. And they took their bones, and buried them under a tree at Jabesh, and fasted seven days.

23. It was round about eighteen thousand measures; and the name of the city from that day shall be, The Lord is there.

24. To the only wise God our Savior, be glory and majesty, dominion and power, both now and ever. Amen.

25. And he shall turn the heart of the fathers to the children, and the heart of the children to their fathers, lest I come and smite the earth with a curse.

26. Greet ye one another with a kiss of charity. Peace be with you all that are in Christ Jesus. Amen.

27. These are the commandments and the judgments, which the Lord commanded by the hand of Moses unto the children of Israel in the plains of Moab by Jordan near Jericho.

28. Make haste, my beloved, and be thou like to a roe or to a young hart upon the mountains of spices.

29. For I will cleanse their blood that I have not cleansed; for the Lord dwelleth in Zion.

30. The Lord Jesus Christ be with thy spirit. Grace be with you. Amen.

18. 3 John
19. 1 Chronicles
20. Mark. (This is probably the real ending of Mark. Many Bibles include verses 9-20, the longer ending.)
21. Exodus
22. 1 Samuel
23. Ezekiel
24. Jude
25. Malachi
26. 1 Peter
27. Numbers
28. Song of Solomon
29. Joel
30. 2 Timothy

31. Let him know, that he which converteth the sinner
    from the error of his way, shall save a soul from
    death, and shall hide a multitude of sins.
32. The grace of the Lord Jesus Christ, and the love of
    God, and the communion of the Holy Ghost, be with
    you all. Amen.
33. Thou wilt perform the truth to Jacob, and the mercy
    to Abraham, which thou hast sworn unto our fathers
    from the days of old.
34. And saviors shall come up on mount Zion to judge
    the mount of Esau; and the kingdom shall be the
    Lord's.
35. All these had taken strange wives; and some of them
    had wives by whom they had children.
36. And his allowance was a continual allowance given
    him of the king, a daily rate for every day, all the
    days of his life.
37. And in that day there shall be no more Canaanite in
    the house of the Lord of hosts.
38. In those days there was no king in Israel; every man
    did that which was right in his own eyes.
39. But grow in grace, and in the knowledge of our Lord
    and Savior Jesus Christ. To him be glory both now
    and forever. Amen.
40. And Obed begat Jesse, and Jesse begat David.
41. These are the commandments, which the Lord
    commanded Moses for the children of Israel in
    Mount Sinai.
42. And there are also many other things which Jesus
    did, the which, if they should be written every one, I
    suppose that even the world itself could not contain
    the books that should be written. Amen.
43. Little children, keep yourselves from idols. Amen.
44. Who is there among you of all his people? The Lord
    his God be with him, and let him go up.

31. James
32. 2 Corinthians
33. Micah
34. Obadiah
35. Ezra
36. 2 Kings
37. Zechariah
38. Judges
39. 2 Peter
40. Ruth
41. Leviticus
42. John
43. 1 John
44. 2 Chronicles

45. There is no healing of thy bruise; thy wound is grievous; all that hear the bruit of thee shall clap the hands over thee; for upon whom hath not thy wickedness passed continually?

46. Brethren, the grace of our Lord Jesus Christ be with your spirit. Amen.

47. Which some professing have erred concerning the faith. Grace be with thee. Amen.

48. And I will plant them upon their land, and they shall no more be pulled up out of their land which I have given them, saith the Lord thy God.

49. So Job died, being old and full of days.

50. Who is wise, and he shall understand these things? prudent, and he shall know them? for the ways of the Lord are right, and the just shall walk in them; but the transgressors shall fall therein.

51. And in all that mighty hand, and in all the great terror which Moses showed in the sight of all Israel.

52. And should I not spare Nineveh, that great city, wherein are more than sixscore thousand persons that cannot discern between their right hand and their left hand; and also much cattle?

53. Preaching the kingdom of God, and teaching those things which concern the Lord Jesus Christ, with all confidence, no man forbidding him.

54. The Lord God is my strength, and he will make my feet like hinds' feet, and he will make me to walk upon mine high places.

55. The children of thy elect sister greet thee. Amen.

56. In that day, saith the Lord of hosts, will I take thee, O Zerubbabel, my servant, the son of Shealtiel, saith the Lord, and will make thee as a signet; for I have chosen thee, saith the Lord of hosts.

57. My love be with you all in Christ Jesus. Amen.

58. For Mordecai the Jew was next unto King Ahasuerus, and great among the Jews, and accepted of the multitude of his brethren, seeking the wealth of his people, and speaking peace to all his seed.

45. Nahum
46. Galatians
47. 1 Timothy
48. Amos
49. Job
50. Hosea
51. Deuteronomy
52. Jonah
53. Acts
54. Habakkuk
55. 2 John
56. Haggai
57. 1 Corinthians
58. Esther

59. Grace be with all them that love our Lord Jesus Christ in sincerity. Amen.
60. Teaching them to observe all things whatsoever I have commanded you; and, lo, I am with you alway, even unto the end of the world. Amen.

✦The Old Testament in the New (II)

Here are more passages from the New Testament, each of them a quotation from the Old Testament. Name the Old Testament book (and, if you're sharp, chapter and verse) where the passage appears.

1. "Thou art my Son, this day have I begotten thee" (Acts 13:33).
2. "Thou shalt not suffer thine Holy One to see corruption" (Acts 13:35).
3. "After this I will return, and will build again the tabernacle of David, which is fallen down; and I will build again the ruins thereof, and I will set it up" (Acts 15:16).
4. "Go unto this people, and say, Hearing ye shall hear, and shall not understand; and seeing ye shall see, and not perceive" (Acts 28:26).
5. "For the name of God is blasphemed among the Gentiles through you, as it is written" (Romans 2:24).
6. "That thou mightest be justified in thy sayings, and mightest overcome when thou art judged" (Romans 3:4).
7. "They are all gone out of the way, they are together become unprofitable; there is none that doeth good, no, not one" (Romans 3:12).
8. "Their throat is an open sepulchre; with their tongues they have used deceit; the poison of asps is under their lips" (Romans 3:13).

59. Ephesians
60. Matthew

✦The Old Testament in the New (II) (Answers)

1. Psalm 2:7
2. Psalm 16:10
3. Amos 9:11
4. Isaiah 6:9
5. Isaiah 52:5
6. Psalm 51:4
7. Psalm 14:3
8. Psalm 5:9

9. "Whose mouth is full of cursing and bitterness" (Romans 3:14).

10. "Their feet are swift to shed blood" (Romans 3:15).

11. "For thy sake we are killed all the day long; we are accounted as sheep for the slaughter" (Romans 8:36).

12. "Jacob have I loved, but Esau have I hated" (Romans 9:13).

13. "I will have mercy on whom I will have mercy, and I will have compassion on whom I will have compassion" (Romans 9:15).

14. "Even for this same purpose have I raised thee up, that I might show my power in thee, that my name might be declared throughout all the earth" (Romans 9:17).

15. "Shall the thing formed say to him that formed it, Why hast thou made me thus?" (Romans 9:20).

16. "I will call them my people, which were not my people; and her beloved, which was not beloved" (Romans 9:25).

17. "Though the number of the children be as the sand of the sea, a remnant shall be saved" (Romans 9:27).

18. "Except the Lord of Sabaoth had left us a seed, we had been as Sodoma, and been made like unto Gomorrha" (Romans 9:29).

19. "Behold, I lay in Zion a stumblingstone and rock of offense; and whosoever believeth on him shall not be ashamed" (Romans 9:33).

20. "Whosoever believeth on him shall not be ashamed" (Romans 10:11).

21. "Lord, who hath believed our report?" (Romans 10:16).

22. "I will provoke you to jealousy by them that are no people, and by a foolish nation I will anger you" (Romans 10:19).

23. "I was found of them that sought me not; I was made manifest unto them that asked not after me" (Romans 10:20).

9. Psalm 10:17
10. Isaiah 59:7
11. Psalm 44:22
12. Malachi 1:2-3
13. Exodus 33:19
14. Exodus 9:16
15. Isaiah 29:16
16. Hosea 2:23
17. Isaiah 10:22
18. Isaiah 13:19
19. Isaiah 28:16
20. Isaiah 28:16
21. Isaiah 53:1
22. Deuteronomy 32:21
23. Isaiah 65:1

24. "All day long I have stretched forth my hands unto a disobedient and gainsaying people" (Romans 10:21).
25. "Hath God cast away his people?" (Romans 11:1).
26. "Lord, they have killed thy prophets, and digged down thine altars; and I am left alone, and they seek my life" (Romans 11:3).
27. "I have reserved to myself seven thousand men, who have not bowed the knee to the image of Baal" (Romans 11:4).
28. "God hath given them the spirit of slumber, eyes that they should not see, and ears that they should not hear" (Romans 11:8).
29. "Let their table be a snare and a trap, and a stumblingblock, and a recompense unto them. Let their eyes be darkened, that they may not see, and bow down their back always" (Romans 11:9-10).
30. "There shall come out of Zion the Deliverer, and shall turn away ungodliness from Jacob. For this is my covenant unto them, when I shall take away their sins" (Romans 11:26-27).
31. "For who hath known the mind of the Lord? or who hath been his counselor?" (Romans 11:34).
32. "Or who hath first given to him, and it shall be recompensed unto him again?" (Romans 11:35).
33. "Vengeance is mine; I will repay" (Romans 12:19).
34. "Therefore if thine enemy hunger, feed him: if he thirst, give him drink: for in so doing thou shalt heap coals of fire on his head" (Romans 12:20).
35. "As I live, saith the Lord, every knee shall bow to me, and every tongue shall confess to God" (Romans 14:11).
36. "The reproaches of them that reproached thee fell on me" (Romans 15:3).
37. "For this cause I will confess to thee among the Gentiles, and sing unto thy name" (Romans 15:9).
38. "Rejoice, ye Gentiles, with his people" (Romans 15:10).

24. Isaiah 65:2
25. Psalm 94:4
26. 1 Kings 19:10, 14
27. 1 Kings 19:18
28. Isaiah 29:10
29. Psalm 69:22-23
30. Isaiah 27:9
31. Isaiah 40:13
32. Job 41:11
33. Deuteronomy 32:35
34. Proverbs 25:21-22
35. Isaiah 45:23
36. Psalm 69:9
37. Psalm 18:50
38. Deuteronomy 32:43

39. "Praise the Lord, all ye Gentiles, and laud him, all ye people" (Romans 15:11).

40. "There shall be a root of Jesse, and he that shall rise to reign over the Gentiles; in him shall the Gentiles trust" (Romans 15:12).

41. "To whom he was not spoken of, they shall see: and they that have not heard shall understand" (Romans 15:21).

42. "I will destroy the wisdom of the wise, and will bring to nothing the understanding of the prudent" (1 Corinthians 1:19).

43. "Where is the wise? where is the scribe? where is the disputer of this world? hath not God made foolish the wisdom of this world?" (1 Corinthians 1:20).

44. "He that glorieth, let him glory in the Lord" (1 Corinthians 1:31).

45. "Eye hath not seen, not ear heard, neither have entered into the heart of man, the things which God hath prepared for them that love him" (1 Corinthians 2:9).

46. "Who hath known the mind of the Lord, that he may instruct him?" (1 Corinthians 2:16).

47. "He taketh the wise in their own craftiness" (1 Corinthians 3:19).

48. "The Lord knoweth the thoughts of the wise, that they are vain" (1 Corinthians 3:20).

49. "Therefore put away from among yourselves that wicked person" (1 Corinthians 5:13).

50. "Thou shalt not muzzle the mouth of the ox that treadeth out the corn" (1 Corinthians 9:9).

51. "The people sat down to eat and drink, and rose up to play" (1 Corinthians 10:7).

52. "For the earth is the Lord's, and the fulness thereof" (1 Corinthians 10:26).

53. "With men of other tongues and other lips will I speak unto this people; and yet for all that will they not hear me, saith the Lord" (1 Corinthians 14:21).

39. Psalm 117:1
40. Isaiah 11:10
41. Isaiah 52:15
42. Isaiah 29:14
43. Isaiah 33:18
44. Jeremiah 9:22-23
45. Isaiah 64:4
46. Isaiah 40:13
47. Job 5:13
48. Psalm 94:11
49. Deuteronomy 13:6
50. Deuteronomy 25:4
51. Exodus 32:6
52. Psalm 24:1.
53. Isaiah 28:11-12

54. "Let us eat and drink; for tomorrow we die" (1 Corinthians 15:32).

55. "The first man Adam was made a living soul" (1 Corinthians 15:45).

56. "O death, where is thy sting? O grave, where is thy victory?" (1 Corinthians 15:55).

57. "I believed, and therefore have I spoken" (2 Corinthians 4:13).

58. "I have heard thee in a time accepted, and in the day of salvation have I succoured thee; behold, now is the accepted time" (2 Corinthians 6:2).

59. "I will dwell in them, and walk in them; and I will be their God, and they shall be my people" (2 Corinthians 6:16).

60. "Wherefore come out from among them, and be ye separate, saith the Lord, and touch not the unclean thing" (2 Corinthians 6:17).

61. "I will receive you, and will be a Father unto you, and ye shall be my sons and daughters, saith the Lord Almighty" (2 Corinthians 6:17-18).

62. "He that had gathered much had nothing over; and he that had gathered little had not lack" (2 Corinthians 8:15).

63. "God loveth a cheerful giver" (2 Corinthians 9:7).

64. "He hath dispersed abroad; he hath given to the poor: his righteousness remaineth forever" (2 Corinthians 9:9).

65. "But he that glorieth, let him glory in the Lord" (2 Corinthians 10:17).

66. "In the mouth of two or three witnesses shall every word be established" (2 Corinthians 13:1).

67. "Abraham believed God, and it was accounted to him for righteousness" (Galatians 3:6).

68. "In thee shall all nations be blessed" (Galatians 3:8).

69. "Cursed is everyone that continueth not in all things which are written in the book of the law to do them" (Galatians 3:10).

70. "The just shall live by faith" (Galatians 3:11).

54. Isaiah 22:13
55. Genesis 2:7
56. Hosea 13:14
57. Psalm 116:10
58. Isaiah 49:8
59. Leviticus 26:12; Jeremiah 32:38
60. Isaiah 52:11
61. Isaiah 43:6
62. Exodus 43:6
63. Proverbs 22:8
64. Psalm 112:9
65. Jeremiah 9:23
66. Deuteronomy 19:15
67. Genesis 15:6
68. Genesis 12:3
69. Deuteronomy 27:26
70. Habakkuk 2:4

✦Prophecies of the Messiah

Many passages in the Old Testament are prophecies which were fulfilled by events in Jesus' life. For each event listed here, name the Old Testament book that contains the prophecy of the event.

1. Casting lots for Jesus robe.
2. Jesus' crucifixion with two thieves.
3. The thirty pieces of silver.
4. The virgin birth.
5. Jesus' birth in Bethlehem.
6. Jesus' resurrection.
7. The piercing of Jesus' side with a spear.
8. Not breaking the bones of the crucified Jesus.
9. Betrayal by a close companion.
10. Jesus' entry into Jerusalem on a donkey.
11. Giving vinegar to the crucified Jesus.
12. Jesus, Mary, and Joseph leaving Egypt and returning to Galilee.
13. Speaking in parables.

✦Who Said That? (III)

1. The waters compassed me about, even to the soul; the depth closed me round about, the weeds were wrapped about my head.
2. I know that my redeemer liveth, and that he shall stand at the latter day upon the earth.
3. What meaneth then this bleating of the sheep in mine ears, and the lowing of the oxen which I hear?
4. Surely the Lord is in this place.
5. For in him we live, and move, and have our being.
6. Lord Jesus, receive my spirit.
7. While the child was yet alive, I fasted and wept; for I said, Who can tell whether God will be gracious to me, that the child may live?

✦Prophecies of the Messiah (Answers)

1. Psalm 22:18: "They part my garments among them, and cast lots upon my vesture."
2. Isaiah 53:12: "He was numbered with the transgressors."
3. Zechariah 11:12: "So they weighed for my price thirty pieces of silver."
4. Isaiah 7:14: "Behold, a virgin shall conceive, and bear a son."
5. Micah 5:2: "But thou Bethlehem Ephratah, though thou be little among the thousands of Judah, yet out of thee shall he come forth unto me that is to be ruler in Israel; whose goings forth have been from of old, from everlasting."
6. Psalm 16:10: "For thou wilt not leave my soul in hell; neither wilt thou suffer thine Holy One to see corruption."
7. Zechariah 12:10: "They shall look upon me whom they have pierced."
8. Psalm 34:20: "He keepeth all his bones; not one of them is broken."
9. Psalm 41:9: "Yea, mine own familiar friend, in whom I trusted, which did eat of my bread, hath lifted up his heel against me."
10. Zechariah 9:9: "Behold, thy king cometh unto thee . . . lowly, and riding upon an ass, and upon a colt the foal of an ass."
11. Psalm 69:21: "In my thirst they gave me vinegar to drink."
12. Hosea 11:1: "I . . . called my son out of Egypt."
13. Psalm 78:2: "I will open my mouth in a parable."

✦Who Said That? (III) (Answers)

1. Jonah (2:5)
2. Job (19:25)
3. Samuel (1 Samuel 15:14)
4. Jacob (Genesis 28:16)
5. Paul (Acts 17:28)
6. Stephen (Acts 7:59)
7. David (2 Samuel 12:22)

8. Where thou diest, will I die, and there will I be buried; the Lord do so to me, and more also, if aught but death part thee and me.

9. Within three days ye shall pass over this Jordan, to go in to possess the land, which the Lord your God giveth you to possess it.

10. This is none other but the house of God, and this is the gate of heaven.

11. It was not you that sent me hither, but God; and he hath made me a father to Pharaoh.

12. Be sure your sin will find you out.

13. Shall not the judge of all the earth do right?

14. God forbid that I should sin against the Lord in ceasing to pray for you.

15. Be thou strong, therefore, and show thyself a man; and keep the charge of the Lord thy God, to walk in his ways.

16. Hear, O Israel: The Lord our God is one Lord.

17. Lord, increase our faith.

18. O earth, earth, earth, hear the word of the Lord.

19. If a man die, shall he live again?

20. Lord, it is nothing with thee to help, whether with many, or with them that have no power; help us, O Lord our God.

21. All things come of thee, and of thine own have we given thee.

22. There hath not failed one word of all his good promise, which he promised by the hand of Moses his servant.

23. For the Lord thy God is a consuming fire, even a jealous God.

24. But as for you, ye thought evil against me, but God meant it unto good, to bring to pass, as it is this day, to save much people alive.

25. We are journeying unto the place of which Lord said, I will give it you. Come thou with us, and we will do thee good; for the Lord hath spoken good concerning Israel.

---

8. Ruth (1:17)
9. Joshua (1:11)
10. Jacob (Genesis 28:17)
11. Joseph (Genesis 45:8)
12. Moses (Numbers 32:23)
13. Abraham (Genesis 18:15)
14. Samuel (1 Samuel 12:23)
15. David (1 Kings 2:2-3)
16. Moses (Deuteronomy 6:4)
17. The disciples (Luke 17:5)
18. Jeremiah (22:29)
19. Job (14:14)
20. Asa (2 Chronicles 14:11)
21. David (1 Chronicles 29:14)
22. Solomon (1 Kings 8:56)
23. Moses (Deuteronomy 4:24)
24. Joseph (Genesis 50:20)
25. Moses (Numbers 10:29)

26. O our God, wilt thou not judge them? For we have no might against this great company that cometh against us; neither know we what to do; but our eyes are upon thee.
27. Though he slay me, yet will I trust in him; but I will maintain mine own ways before him.
28. Is there no balm in Gilead? Is there no physician there?
29. Woe to them that are at ease in Zion.
30. For the earth shall be filled with the knowledge of the glory of the Lord, as the waters cover the sea.
31. And now brethren, I commend you to God, and to the word of his grace, which is able to build you up, among all them which are sanctified.
32. Not by might, nor by power, but by my spirit, saith the Lord of hosts.
33. And it shall come to pass afterward, that I will pour out my spirit upon all flesh.
34. He hath showed thee, O man, what is good; and what doth the Lord require of thee, but to do justly, and to love mercy, and to walk humbly with thy God?
35. Believe in the Lord your God, so shall ye be established; believe his prophets, so shall ye prosper.
36. For the Lord searcheth all hearts, and understandeth all the imaginations of the thoughts; if thou seek him, he will be found of thee.
37. The grass withereth, the flower fadeth, but the word of our God shall stand forever.
38. Behold, I will send you Elijah the prophet before the coming of the great and dreadful day of the Lord.
39. This is the stone which was set at nought of you builders, which is become the head of the corner.
40. Let judgment run down as waters, and righteousness as a mighty stream.
41. Seek good, and not evil, that ye may live; and so the Lord, the God of hosts, shall be with you.

26. Jehoshaphat (2 Chronicles 20:12)
27. Job (13:15)
28. Jeremiah (8:22)
29. Amos (6:1)
30. Habakkuk (2:14)
31. Paul (Acts 20:32)
32. Zechariah (4:6)
33. Joel (2:28)
34. Micah (6:8)
35. Jehoshaphat (2 Chronicles 20:20)
36. David (1 Chronicles 28:9)
37. Isaiah (40:8)
38. Malachi (4:5)
39. Peter (Acts 4:11)
40. Amos (5:24)
41. Amos (5:14)

42. Daughter, be of good comfort; thy faith hath made thee whole.

43. Am I not a Benjaminite, of the smallest of the tribes of Israel?

44. But, behold, they will not believe me, nor hearken unto my voice; for they will say, The Lord hath not appeared unto thee.

45. Come near now, and kiss me, my son.

46. What is this dream that thou hast dreamed? Shall I and thy mother and thy brethren indeed come to bow down ourselves to thee to the earth?

47. I did see Israel scattered upon the mountains, as sheep that have no shepherd; and the Lord said, These have no master.

48. God forbid that I should justify you; till I die I will not remove mine integrity from me.

49. We will go with our young and with our old, with our sons and with our daughters, with our flocks and with our herds will we go; for we must hold a feast unto the Lord.

50. If thou be the king of the Jews, save thyself.

51. Behold, I will send you Elijah the prophet before the coming of the great and dreadful day of the Lord.

52. Ho, everyone that thirsteth, come ye to the waters, and he that hath no money; come ye, buy, and eat.

53. Yet once, it is a little while, and I will shake the heavens, and the earth, and the sea, and the dry land.

54. Whether it be right in the sight of God to hearken unto you more than unto God, judge ye.

55. How beautiful upon the mountains are the feet of him that bringeth good tidings, that publisheth peace.

56. Who am I? And what is my life, or my father's family in Israel, that I should be son-in-law to the king?

57. Give me children, or else I die.

58. What will ye then that I shall do unto him whom ye call the King of the Jews?

42. Jesus (Matthew 9:22)
43. Saul (1 Samuel 9:21)
44. Moses (Exodus 4:1)
45. Isaac (Genesis 27:26)
46. Jacob (Genesis 37:10)
47. Micaiah (2 Chronicles 18:16)
48. Job (27:5)
49. Moses (Exodus 10:9)
50. The soldiers at the Crucifixion (Luke 23:37)
51. Malachi (4:5)
52. Isaiah (55:1)
53. Haggai (2:6)
54. Peter and John (Acts 4:19)
55. Isaiah (52:7)
56. David (1 Samuel 18:18)
57. Rachel (Genesis 30:1)
58. Pilate (Mark 15:12)

59. Behold my servant whom I uphold; my elect, in whom my soul delighteth; I have put my spirit upon him.

60. Come and let us return unto the Lord; for he hath torn, and he will heal us; he hath smitten, and he will bind us up.

◆The Old Testament in the New (III)

Here are still more passages from the New Testament, each of them a quotation from the Old Testament. Name the Old Testament book (and, if you're sharp, chapter and verse) where the passage appears.

1. "Cursed is everyone one that hangeth on a tree" (Galatians 3:13).

2. "The man that doeth them shall live in them" (Galatians 3:12).

3. "Rejoice, thou barren that bearest not; break forth and cry, thou that travailest not: for the desolate hath many more children than she which hath a husband" (Galatians 4:27).

4. "Cast out the bondwoman and her son: for the son of the bondwoman shall not be heir with the son of the freewoman" (Galatians 4:30).

5. "And [he] hath put all things under his feet" (Ephesians 1:22).

6. "And [he] came and preached peace to you who were afar off, and to them that were nigh" (Ephesians 2:17).

7. "When he ascended up on high, he led captivity captive, and gave gifts unto men" (Ephesians 4:8).

8. "Speak every man truth with his neighbor" (Ephesians 4:25).

9. "Be ye angry, and sin not" (Ephesians 4:26).

59. Isaiah (42:1)
60. Hosea (6:1)

✦The Old Testament in the New (III) (Answers)

1. Deuteronomy 21:23
2. Leviticus 18:5
3. Isaiah 54:1
4. Genesis 21:10
5. Psalm 8:6
6. Isaiah 57:19
7. Psalm 68:18
8. Zechariah 8:16
9. Psalm 4:4

10. "For this cause shall a man leave his father and mother, and shall be joined unto his wife, and they two shall be one flesh" (Ephesians 5:31).

11. "Honor thy father and mother: which is the first commandment with promise; that it may be well with thee, and thou mayest live long on the earth" (Ephesians 6:2-3).

12. "The Lord knoweth them that are his" (2 Timothy 2:19).

13. "Thou art my Son, this day have I begotten thee" (Hebrews 1:5).

14. "I will be to him a Father, and he shall be to me a Son?" (Hebrews 1:5).

15. "Let all the angels of God worship him" (Hebrews 1:6).

16. "Who maketh his angels spirits, and his ministers a flame of fire" (Hebrews 1:7).

17. "Thy throne, O God, is for ever and ever: a sceptre of righteousness is the sceptre of thy kingdom. Thou hast loved righteousness, and hated iniquity; therefore God, even thy God, hath anointed thee with the oil of gladness above thy fellows" (Hebrews 1:8-9).

18. "Thou, Lord, in the beginning hast laid the foundation of the earth; and the heavens are the works of thine hands" (Hebrews 1:10).

19. "They shall perish, but thou remainest; and they all shall wax old as doth a garment" (Hebrews 1:11).

20. "But thou art the same, and thy years shall not fail" (Hebrews 1:12).

21. "What is man, that thou art mindful of him? or the son of man, that thou visitest him?" (Hebrews 2:6).

22. "Thou hast put all things in subjection under his feet" (Hebrews 2:8).

23. "I will declare thy name unto my brethren, in the midst of the church will I sing praise unto thee" (Hebrews 2:12).

24. "I will put my trust in him" (Hebrews 2:13).

10. Genesis 2:24
11. Deuteronomy 5:16
12. Numbers 16:15
13. Psalm 2:7
14. 2 Samuel 7:14
15. Deuteronomy 32:43
16. Psalm 104:4
17. Psalm 45:6-7
18. Psalm 102:25
19. Psalm 102:26
20. Psalm 102:27
21. Psalm 8:4
22. Psalm 8:6
23. Psalm 22:22
24. Isaiah 8:17

25. "Behold I and the children which God hath given me" (Hebrews 2:13).

26. "Today if ye will hear his voice, harden not your hearts, as in the provocation, in the day of temptation in the wilderness" (Hebrews 3:7-8).

27. "Wherefore I was grieved with that generation, and said, They do always err in their heart; and they have not known my ways" (Hebrews 3:10).

28. "And God did rest the seventh day from all his works" (Hebrews 4:4).

29. "Thou art a priest forever after the order of Melkizedek" (Hebrews 5:6).

30. "Surely blessing I will bless thee, and multiplying I will multiply thee" (Hebrews 6:14).

31. "I will put my laws into their mind, and write them in their hearts" (Hebrews 8:10).

32. "And they shall not teach every man his neighbour, and every man his brother, saying, Know the Lord: for all shall know me" (Hebrews 8:11).

33. "This is the blood of the testament which God hath enjoined unto you" (Hebrews 9:20).

34. "Sacrifice and offering thou wouldest not, but a body hast thou prepared for me: in burnt offerings and sacrifices for sin thou hast had no pleasure" (Hebrews 10:5-6).

35. "Then said he, Lo, I come to do thy will, O God" (Hebrews 10:9).

36. "Vengeance belongeth unto me, I will recompense, saith the Lord" (Hebrews 10:30).

37. "The Lord shall judge his people" (Hebrews 10:30).

38. "In Isaac shall thy seed be called" (Hebrews 11:18).

39. "My son, despise not thou the chastening of the Lord, nor faint when thou art rebuked of him; for whom the Lord loveth he chasteneth" (Hebrews 12:5-6).

40. "Wherefore lift up the hands which hang down, and the feeble knees" (Hebrews 12:12).

25. Isaiah 8:18
26. Psalm 95:7-8
27. Psalm 95:10
28. Genesis 2:2
29. Psalm 110:4
30. Genesis 22:17
31. Jeremiah 31:33
32. Jeremiah 31:34
33. Exodus 24:8
34. Psalm 40:6
35. Psalm 40:7-8
36. Deuteronomy 32:35
37. Deuteronomy 32:36
38. Genesis 21:12
39. Proverbs 3:11-12
40. Isaiah 35:3

41. "Make straight paths for your feet" (Hebrews 12:13).

42. "Yet once more I shake not the earth only, but also heaven" (Hebrews 12:26).

43. "I will never leave thee, nor forsake thee" (Hebrews 13:5).

44. "The Lord is my helper, and I will not fear what man shall do unto me" (Hebrews 13:6).

45. "Abraham believed God, and it was imputed unto him for righteousness" (James 2:23).

46. "God resisteth the proud, but giveth grace unto the humble" (James 4:6).

47. "Be ye holy; for I am holy" (1 Peter 1:16).

48. "For all flesh is grass, and all the glory of man as the flower of grass. The grass withereth, and the flower thereof falleth away: but the word of the Lord endureth forever" (1 Peter 1:24–25).

49. "Behold, I lay in Zion a chief corner stone, elect, precious" (1 Peter 2:6).

50. "A stone of stumbling, and a rock of offense" (1 Peter 2:8).

51. "Who did not sin, neither was any guile found in his mouth" (1 Peter 2:22).

52. "For he that will love life, and see good days, let him refrain his tongue from evil, and his lips that they speak no guile" (1 Peter 3:10).

53. "Let him eschew evil, and do good" (1 Peter 3:11).

54. "The eyes of the Lord are over the righteous, and his ears are open unto their prayers: but the face of the Lord is against them that do evil" (1 Peter 3:12).

55. "Be not afraid of their terror, neither be troubled" (1 Peter 3:14).

56. "If the righteous scarcely be saved, where shall the ungodly and the sinner appear?" (1 Peter 4:18).

57. "The dog is turned to his own vomit again" (2 Peter 2:22).

58. "One day is with the Lord as a thousand years, and a thousand years as one day" (2 Peter 3:8).

41. Proverbs 4:26
42. Haggai 2:6
43. Deuteronomy 31:6
44. Psalm 118:6
45. Genesis 15:16
46. Proverbs 3:34
47. Leviticus 19:2
48. Isaiah 40:6-8
49. Isaiah 28:16
50. Isaiah 8:14
51. Isaiah 53:9
52. Psalm 34:12-13
53. Psalm 34:14
54. Psalm 34:15-16
55. Isaiah 8:12-13
56. Proverbs 11:31
57. Proverbs 26:11
58. Psalm 90:4

59. "And he shall rule them with a rod of iron; as the vessels of a potter shall they be broken to shivers" (Revelation 2:27).

60. "And let him that is athirst come" (Revelation 22:17).

◆The Last Word

Name the persons who said the following as their last words.

1. Lord Jesus, receive my spirit. Lord, lay not this sin to their charge.

2. There they buried Abraham and Sarah his wife; there they buried Isaac and Rebekah his wife; and there I buried Leah.

3. Thou shouldest have smitten five or six times; then hadst thou smitten Syria till thou hadst consumed it; whereas now thou shalt smite Syria but thrice.

4. Draw thy sword, and thrust me through therewith; lest these uncircumcised come and thrust me through, and abuse me.

5. God will surely visit you, and ye shall carry up my bones from hence.

6. Happy art thou, O Israel, who is like unto thee, O people saved by the Lord, the shield of thy help, and who is the sword of thy excellency! And thine enemies shall be found liars unto thee; and thou shalt tread upon their high places.

7. Behold, this stone shall be a witness unto us; for it hath heard all the words of the Lord which he spake unto us; it shall be therefore a witness unto you, lest ye deny your God.

8. O Lord GOD, remember me, I pray thee, and strengthen me, I pray thee, only this once, O God, that I may be at once avenged of the Philistines for my two eyes.

59. Psalm 2:9
60. Isaiah 55:1

✦The Last Word (Answers)

1. Stephen (Acts 7:59-60)
2. Jacob (Genesis 49:31)
3. Elisha (2 Kings 13:19)
4. Saul (1 Samuel 31:4)
5. Joseph (Genesis 50:25)
6. Moses (Deuteronomy 33:29)
7. Joshua (Joshua 24:27)
8. Samson (Judges 16:28)

9. Go ye therefore, and teach all nations, baptizing them in the name of the Father, and of the Son, and of the Holy Ghost, teaching them to observe all things whatsoever I have commanded you; and, lo, I am with you alway, even unto the end of the world.

10. Lord, remember me when thou comest into thy kingdom.

11. Now therefore hold him not guiltless; for thou art a wise man, and knowest what thou oughtest to do unto him; but his hoar head bring thou down to the grave with blood.

12. What is there done, my son?

13. But ye shall receive power, after that the Holy Ghost is come upon you; and ye shall be witnesses unto me, both in Jerusalem, and in all Judea, and in Samaria, and unto the uttermost part of the earth.

14. Thou hast asked a hard thing; nevertheless, if thou see me when I am taken from thee, it shall be so unto thee; but if not, it shall not be so.

15. Had Zimri peace, who slew his master?

16. Come to me, and I will give thy flesh unto the fowls of the air and to the beasts of the field.

17. Turn thine hand, and carry me out of the host; for I am wounded.

18. They shall take up serpents; and if they drink any deadly thing, it shall not hurt them; they shall lay hands on the sick, and they shall recover.

◆Who Said That? (IV)

1. Jesus Christ maketh thee whole; arise, and make thy bed.

2. Why is my pain perpetual, and my wound incurable, which refuseth to be healed?

9. Jesus (Matthew 28:19-20)
10. The repentant thief on the cross (Luke 23:42)
11. David (1 Kings 2:9)
12. Eli (1 Samuel 4:16)
13. Jesus (Acts 1:8)
14. Elijah (2 Kings 2:10)
15. Jezebel (2 Kings 9:31)
16. Goliath (1 Samuel 17:44)
17. Ahab (1 Kings 22:34)
18. Jesus (Mark 16:18)

✦Who Said That? (IV) (Answers)

1. Peter (Acts 9:34)
2. Jeremiah (15:18)

3. And after thee shall arise another kingdom inferior to thee, and another third kingdom of brass, which shall bear rule over all the earth.

4. We have found him, of whom Moses in the law, and the prophets, did write, Jesus of Nazareth, the son of Joseph.

5. Do violence to no man, neither accuse any falsely; and be content with your wages.

6. In the name of Jesus Christ of Nazareth rise up and walk.

7. What I have written, I have written.

8. A man can receive nothing, except it be given him from heaven.

9. God hath numbered thy kingdom, and finished it.

10. But the Lord is in his holy temple; let all the earth keep silence before him.

11. Thy crowned are as the locusts, and thy captains as the great grasshoppers.

12. Lord, trouble not thyself; for I am not worthy that thou shouldest enter under my roof.

13. Will a man rob God?

14. Woe to them that devise iniquity, and work evil upon their beds!

15. My mother and my brethren are these which hear the word of God, and do it.

16. I shall now perish one day by the hand of Saul.

17. Hast thou found me, O mine enemy?

18. Can two walk together, except they be agreed?

19. Sir, I perceive that thou art a prophet.

20. Son, why hast thou thus dealt with us? Behold, thy father and I have sought thee sorrowing.

21. Let us now go even unto Bethlehem, and see this thing which is come to pass, which the Lord hath made known unto us.

22. He shall speak peace unto the heathen; and his dominion shall be from sea even to sea.

3. Daniel (2:39)
4. Philip (John 1:45)
5. John the Baptist (Luke 3:14)
6. Peter (Acts 3:6)
7. Pilate (John 19:22)
8. John the Baptist (John 3:27)
9. Daniel (5:26)
10. Habakkuk (2:20)
11. Nahum (3:17)
12. The centurion of Capernaum (Luke 7:6)
13. Malachi (3:8)
14. Micah (2:1)
15. Jesus (Luke 8:21)
16. David (1 Samuel 27:1)
17. Ahab (1 Kings 21:20)
18. Amos (3:3)
19. The woman at the well (John 4:19)
20. Mary (Luke 2:48)
21. The shepherds (Luke 2:15)
22. Zechariah (9:10)

23. Why have I found grace in thine eyes, that thou shouldest take knowledge of me, seeing I am a stranger?

24. Have pity upon me, have pity upon me, O ye my friends; for the hand of God hath touched me.

25. But thou Bethlehem Ephratah, though thou be little among the thousands of Judah, yet out of thee shall he come forth unto me that is to be ruler in Israel.

26. Thou art the Christ, the Son of the living God.

27. At midday, O king, I saw in the way a light from heaven, above the brightness of the sun, shining round about me and them which journeyed with me.

28. As many as I love, I rebuke and chasten; be zealous therefore, and repent.

29. Happy art thou, O Israel; who is like unto thee, O people saved by the Lord, the shield of thy help, and who is the sword of thy excellency!

30. Sing ye to the Lord, for he hath triumphed gloriously; the horse and his rider hath he thrown into the sea.

31. Lord, speakest thou this parable unto us, or even to all?

32. The voice of him that crieth in the wilderness, Prepare ye the way of the Lord, make straight in the desert a highway for our God.

33. Behold, the days come, saith the Lord, that I will sow the house of Israel and the house of Judah with the seed of man, and with the seed of beast.

34. Understandest thou what thou readest?

35. Thy money perish with thee, because thou hast thought that the gift of God may be purchased with money.

36. Which of the prophets have not your fathers persecuted?

37. Hate the evil, and love the good, and establish judgment in the gate; it may be that the Lord God of hosts will be gracious unto the remnant of Jacob.

38. Our father is old, and there is not a man in the earth to come in unto us after the manner of all the earth.

23. Ruth (2:10)
24. Job (19:21)
25. Micah (5:2)
26. Peter (Matthew 16:16)
27. Paul (Acts 26:13)
28. Jesus (Revelation 3:19)
29. Moses (Deuteronomy 33:29)
30. Miriam (Exodus 15:21)
31. Peter (Luke 12:41)
32. Isaiah (40:3)
33. Jeremiah (31:27)
34. Philip (Acts 8:30)
35. Peter (Acts 8:20)
36. Stephen (Acts 7:52)
37. Amos (5:15)
38. Lot's daughters (Genesis 19:31)

39. Hath Amnon thy brother been with thee?
40. Is there not an appointed time to man upon earth? Are not his days also like the days of a hireling?
41. I have sinned in that I have betrayed the innocent blood.
42. A prophet is not without honor, save in his own country, and in his own house.
43. Ye men of Israel, why marvel ye at this? Or why look ye so earnestly on us, as though by our own power or holiness we had made this man to walk?
44. Bring me up Samuel.
45. For God doth know that in the day ye eat thereof, then your eyes shall be opened, and ye shall be as gods, knowing good and evil.
46. What evil hath he done? I have found no cause of death in him; I will therefore chastise him and let him go.
47. Whomsoever I shall kiss, that same is he; take him, and lead him away safely.
48. Art thou he that troubleth Israel?
49. Behold, the nations are as a drop of a bucket, and are counted as the small dust of the balance.
50. Lord, how is it that thou wilt manifest thyself unto us, and not unto the world?

39. Absalom (2 Samuel 13:20)
40. Job (7:1)
41. Judas Iscariot (Matthew 27:4)
42. Jesus (Matthew 13:57)
43. Peter (Acts 3:12)
44. Saul (1 Samuel 28:11)
45. The serpent (Genesis 3:5)
46. Pilate (Luke 23:22)
47. Judas Iscariot (Mark 14:44)
48. Ahab (1 Kings 18:17)
49. Isaiah (40:15)
50. Judas (not Iscariot) (John 14:22)

PART 6
Books, Authors, Translators

✦So Many Versions

1. What book, published in its entirety in 1971, has been the best-selling paraphrase of the Holy Bible?
2. What translation, popular with contemporary evangelicals, was done under the auspices of the New York International Bible Society and published in 1978?
3. What famous Greek version of the Old Testament, usually designated by LXX, was supposed to have been completed by seventy scholars working in Alexandria, Egypt, around 250 B.C.?
4. What are the oldest existing copies of pieces of several Old Testament books called?
5. What Bible, now in the British Museum, is the oldest complete Bible in existence?
6. What famous church scholar made the much-used Latin translation known as the Vulgate?
7. What king of England and Scotland authorized a translation of the Bible that was published in 1611?
8. What, until recent years, was the most popular English Bible used by Roman Catholics?
9. What is the alternate title of the American Bible Society's translation Today's English Version?
10. What medieval Englishman translated the Latin Bible's New Testament into English and encouraged further translation work?
11. What large English Bible, published in 1539, was chained to the reading desk in English churches?

✦So Many Versions (Answers)

1. *The Living Bible*
2. The New International Version
3. The Septuagint
4. The Dead Sea Scrolls
5. Codex Sinaiticus
6. Jerome
7. James I
8. The Douay Version
9. The Good News Bible
10. John Wycliffe
11. The Great Bible

12. What widely used revision of the King James Version was published in 1952 under the auspices of the International Council of Religious Education?

13. What text of the Old Testament—the first to include vowel markings along with the Hebrew consonants—is considered the authoritative text for most Bible translators?

14. What English translation was made in Europe by scholars who fled the persecution of Protestants under Bloody Mary?

15. When was the New King James Version published?

16. What fresh translation from the Hebrew and Greek was published in 1970 with the assistance of the university presses of Oxford and Cambridge?

17. What English translation, published in 1965, contains bracketed words intended to explain many difficult phrases?

18. What Bible scholar published a translation of Paul's epistles called *Letters to Young Churches*?

19. What Scottish scholar, famous as the author of the *Daily Study Bible,* published his own translation of the New Testament?

20. What English Bible, prepared during the reign of Elizabeth I, was popular with the clergy but not with the common people?

21. What English Catholic did a popular translation of the Bible in the 1940s?

22. What multivolume translation, done by a number of Catholics, Protestants, and Jews, was started in 1964 and is still incomplete?

23. What version, popular with American evangelicals, was sponsored by the Lockman Foundation and published in 1971?

24. What former monk made a translation of the Bible into German that was loved for centuries?

25. What medieval Archbishop of Canterbury is largely responsible for dividing the Bible into chapters?

12. The Revised Standard Version
13. The Masoretic text
14. The Geneva Bible
15. 1982
16. The New English Bible
17. The Amplified Bible
18. J. B. Phillips
19. William Barclay
20. The Bishops' Bible
21. Ronald A. Knox
22. The Anchor Bible
23. The New American Standard Bible
24. Martin Luther
25. Stephen Langton

26. What French Protestant scholar, riding on horseback from Paris to Lyons, divided the New Testament into verses?

27. What English translation, published in 1966, had notes based on a French translation done in Jerusalem?

28. What English translator died as a martyr before he could complete his translation of the Old Testament?

29. What was the name of the New Testament paraphrase, done in the style of Southern black tales, written by Clarence Jordan?

30. What Bible was the one most likely used by Shakespeare, the Pilgrims, and Oliver Cromwell's soldiers?

31. What translation, often called the "Chicago Bible," was completed in 1931 by E. J. Goodspeed, J. M. Powis Smith, and others?

32. What brilliant Dutch scholar produced the *textus receptus,* an edition of the Greek New Testament that was used for centuries as the basis for Bible translating?

33. What modern-day community of Protestant monks in France produced a "picture Bible" for adults?

34. What Bible version was the basis for the King James Version?

35. What was the Complutensian Polyglot?

36. What was Taverner's Bible?

37. When the New King James Version (1982) was repackaged in 1984, what was it called?

38. What is the alternative title of *The Modern Language Bible* (1969)?

39. Who translated *The Holy Bible in the Language of Today: An American Translation* (1976)?

40. What was the first Bible to use italics for explanatory and connective words and phrases?

41. In November 1986, a modern English translation became the first to outsell the King James Version. What was it?

26. Robert Estienne
27. The Jerusalem Bible
28. William Tyndale
29. *The Cotton Patch Version*
30. The Geneva Bible
31. *The Bible: An American Translation*
32. Erasmus
33. Taize
34. The Bishops' Bible (1568)
35. The massive six-volume work, published in Spain in 1513, that contained the Hebrew and Greek texts, the Septuagint, the Vulgate, and the Chaldee paraphrase of the Pentateuch
36. An independent translation made by Greek scholar Richard Taverner in 1539
37. The Bible
38. The New Berkeley Version
39. William Beck
40. The Geneva Bible (1560)
41. The New International Version

42. What much-used version, authorized by the National Council of Churches, aroused controversy when its "de-sexed" revision came out in 1990?
43. What was the Unrighteous Bible?
44. What was the Place-makers' Bible?
45. What was the Discharge Bible?
46. What was the He Bible?
47. What was the Murderers' Bible?
48. What was the Standing Fishes Bible?
49. What was the Wicked Bible?
50. What was the Rosin Bible?
51. What was the Wife-hater Bible?
52. What was the Printers' Bible?
53. What was the Breeches Bible?
54. What was the Bug Bible?
55. What was the Ear to Ear Bible?
56. What were Poor Man's Bibles?
57. What was the Treacle Bible?

42. The Revised Standard Version, now available as the *New Revised Standard Version*. The New RSV left in the male pronouns referring to God but eliminated most instances of *man* that referred to human beings in general.

43. An edition, printed at Cambridge in 1653, containing the printer's error, "Know ye not that the unrighteous shall inherit the kingdom of God?" (1 Corinthians 6:9)

44. The second edition of the Geneva Bible, printed in 1562, which has a printer's error in Matthew 5:9: "Blessed are the place-makers."

45. An 1806 Bible that substituted "discharge" for "charge" in 1 Timothy 5:21: "I discharge thee before God."

46. The first edition of the King James Bible, which (correctly) reads "He went into the city" (Ruth 3:15). Later versions often incorrectly used "she." The verse refers to Boaz.

47. An edition of 1801 which contained this misprint of Jude 16: "There are murderers, complainers, walking after their own lusts." It should read "murmurers."

48. An 1806 printing in which Ezekiel 47:10 reads, "And it shall come to pass that the fishes shall stand upon it." It should read "fishers."

49. A 1632 English Bible that omitted the word "not" in the seventh commandment. It read, "Thou shalt commit adultery."

50. The Catholic Douay Bible, which has for Jeremiah 8:22, "Is there no rosin in Gilead?"

51. An 1810 Bible in which "life" in Luke 14:26 is printed "wife."

52. A 1702 printing which substitutes "printers" for "princes" in Psalm 119:161: "Printers have persecuted me without a cause."

53. The Geneva Bible, so called because Genesis 3:7 reads, "They sewed fig tree leaves together, and made themselves breeches."

54. Coverdale's Bible (1535), which has this translation for Psalm 91:5: "Thou shalt not need to be afraid for any bugs by night." (The King James Version has "terror by night.")

55. An 1810 printing in which Matthew 13:43 reads, "Who hath ears to ear, let him hear."

56. Picture books widely used in the Middle Ages in place of the Bible. Used by the illiterate, they were probably the earliest books to be printed.

57. The Bishops' Bible, so called because Jeremiah 8:22 reads, "Is there no treacle in Gilead?"

◆Author, Author

Who, according to tradition, wrote the following books of the Bible?

1. Exodus
2. Revelation
3. Hebrews
4. Esther
5. Proverbs
6. Ruth
7. 1 and 2 Chronicles
8. Lamentations
9. Song of Songs
10. Numbers
11. Nehemiah
12. Judges
13. Psalms
14. Ecclesiastes
15. Ezra
16. Deuteronomy
17. Job
18. 1 and 2 Kings
19. Leviticus
20. Joshua
21. Acts
22. Jude
23. Genesis
24. 1 and 2 Samuel
25. James

◆Author, Author (Answers)

1. Moses
2. The apostle John
3. Not known, though often attributed to Paul, Apollos, and many others
4. Attributed to Ezra, Mordecai, and others
5. Solomon, although the book itself names other contributors
6. Samuel
7. Ezra
8. Jeremiah
9. Solomon
10. Moses
11. Nehemiah
12. Samuel
13. David, Asaph, and many others
14. Solomon
15. Ezra
16. Moses
17. Moses
18. Jeremiah
19. Moses
20. Joshua
21. Luke
22. Jude, the brother of Jesus
23. Moses
24. Samuel and, possibly, the prophet Nathan
25. James, the brother of Jesus

◆Books within the Book

1. What prophet ate a book and found it sweet as honey?
2. What book of the Bible mentions the Lamb's book of life?
3. Which king's acts are said to be recorded in "the book of Jehu the son of Hanani"?
4. Whose acts are recorded in "the book of Shemaiah the prophet"?
5. Whose acts are recorded in "the book of Iddo the seer"?
6. The "book of Gad the seer" records which king's deeds?
7. King David's acts are said to be recorded in the book of which court prophet?
8. What book of the Bible makes reference to "the books of the chronicles of the kings of Media and Persia"?
9. What New Testament writer ate a book that tasted good but gave him indigestion?
10. What Persian king received a letter, asking him to search through the "book of the records" to remind himself how rebellious the Jews had been?
11. What Old Testament prophet mentions the Lord's "book of remembrance"?
12. According to Revelation, who will open the book with seven seals?
13. What king cut up Jeremiah's scroll and tossed it piece by piece into a fireplace?
14. In what city in Asia did people burn their valuable books on sorcery?
15. What Old Testament book mentions "the book of the acts of Solomon"?
16. Who described to the people of Israel what life would be like under a king, and then wrote down his statements in a book?

◆Books within the Book (Answers)

1. Ezekiel (2:9–3:3)
2. Revelation (21:27)
3. Jehoshaphat (2 Chronicles 20:34)
4. Rehoboam (2 Chronicles 12:15)
5. Rehoboam (2 Chronicles 12:15)
6. David's (1 Chronicles 29:29)
7. Nathan (1 Chronicles 29:29)
8. Esther (10:1-2)
9. John (Revelation 10:9-10)
10. Artaxerxes (Ezra 4:15)
11. Malachi (3:16-17)
12. The lion of the tribe of Judah (Revelation 5:5)
13. Jehoiakim (Jeremiah 36:23)
14. Ephesus (Acts 19:18-19)
15. 1 Kings (11:41)
16. Samuel (1 Samuel 10:25)

17. Who instructed the men of Israel to go through Canaan and write down descriptions of the area?
18. What phenomenal event, described in Joshua, is also said to be described in the "book of Jashar"?
19. What Old Testament book makes reference to "the book of the wars of the Lord"?
20. According to tradition, the "book of the law" found in the temple during Josiah's reign was a form of which Old Testament book?

◆Scripture Translates Itself

In several places Scripture explains the meaning of phrases or the names of certain people and places. For the meanings listed below, supply the proper name.

1. Sons of thunder.
2. God with us.
3. The place of the skull.
4. King of peace.
5. Teacher.
6. Son of encouragement.
7. Sorcerer.
8. Little girl.
9. Be opened.
10. Sent.
11. King of righteousness.
12. Bitter.
13. My God, my God, why have you forsaken me?
14. Confused.
15. Red.
16. Small.
17. Shelters.
18. Burning.
19. Not my people.
20. No more mercy.

17. Joshua (18:9)
18. The sun standing still (Joshua 10:13)
19. Numbers (21:14-15)
20. Deuteronomy

◆Scripture Translates Itself (Answers)

1. Boanerges (Mark 3:17)
2. Immanuel (Matthew 1:23)
3. Golgotha (Matthew 27:33)
4. King of Salem (Hebrews 7:2)
5. Rabboni or Rabbi (John 1:38; 20:16)
6. Barnabas (Acts 4:36)
7. Elymas (Acts 13:8)
8. Talitha (Mark 5:41)
9. Ephphatha (Mark 7:34)
10. Siloam (John 9:7)
11. Melchizedek (Hebrews 7:2)
12. Marah (Exodus 15:23)
13. Eloi, eloi, lama sabachthani (Mark 15:34)
14. Babel (Genesis 11:9)
15. Edom (Genesis 25:30)
16. Zoar (Genesis 19:22)
17. Succoth (Genesis 33:17)
18. Taberah (Numbers 11:3)
19. Lo-Ammi (Hosea 1:9)
20. Lo-Ruhamah (Hosea 1:6)

✦Between the Testaments

Name the books described below. Some are part of the Apocrypha and are regarded as Scripture by Catholics and some others. Some are considered Pseudipigrapha and are not accepted as genuine Scripture by either Jews or Christians. Some are translations or commentaries made (or begun) after the close of the Old Testament.

1. A book of wise sayings attributed to a king of Israel.
2. A romantic story of a pious Jew whose son is aided by the angel Raphael.
3. A tale of a brave Jewish woman who saves her city from the army of Nebuchadnezzar by murdering a Babylonian captain.
4. A book of wisdom whose author is identified in the text as Sirach of Jerusalem.
5. A historical work that recounts the story of the Jewish revolt against the evil ruler Antiochus Epiphanes and his successors.
6. A book of prayers and confessions, supposedly written by the friend of an Old Testament prophet.
7. A tale of a virtuous woman accused of adultery and proved innocent by Daniel.
8. An eloquent prayer reputed to be the work of a repentant king of Judah.
9. A tale of Babylonian idol worship and some conniving priests.
10. A historical work that covers some of the same history chronicled in Ezra, Nehemiah, and 2 Chronicles.
11. This book consists of alleged predictions of Moses, given to Joshua just before Moses' death.
12. These are additions, not found in the Hebrew Bible, to an Old Testament book about the Persian period.
13. This addition to the Book of Daniel contains an eloquent prayer, a miraculous deliverance, and a hymn of praise.

✦Between the Testaments (Answers)

1. Wisdom of Solomon (Apocrypha)
2. Tobit (Apocrypha)
3. Judith (Apocrypha)
4. Ecclesiasticus (Apocrypha)
5. 1 Maccabees (Apocrypha)
6. Baruch (Apocrypha)
7. Susanna (Apocrypha)
8. The Prayer of Manasseh (Apocrypha)
9. Bel and the Dragon (Apocrypha)
10. 1 Esdras (Apocrypha)
11. The Assumption of Moses (Pseudipigrapha)
12. Additions to Esther (Apocrypha)
13. Song of the Three Children (Apocrypha)

14. This work is a shortened form of a five-volume historical work by Jason of Cyrene. It contains letters to the Jews in Egypt.

15. This apocalyptic work contains bizarre visions, images of the Messiah, and references to the Roman Empire.

16. This book about a famous Judean prophet tells of his martyrdom under wicked King Manasseh.

17. These eighteen poems about the coming Messiah are ascribed to a famous Hebrew poet.

18. This collection of predictions speaks about the downfall of empires and the messianic age.

19. This book of revelations purports to have been written by Enoch and Noah.

20. This book purports to be the dying speeches of Jacob's twelve sons.

21. Written by a Pharisee, this book extols the law and the Hebrew patriarchs and urges Jews not to be influenced by Greek culture.

22. These are loose translations of the Hebrew Scriptures into the Aramaic language, made after Aramaic, not Hebrew, was the common language of Palestine.

23. This collection of laws based on the laws of Moses was not completed until A.D. 500. It consists of the Mishnah and the Gemara and is still widely studied by Jewish scholars today.

◆Take a Letter

1. What lost letter of Paul is mentioned in the Letter to the Colossians?

2. Who received a letter from David, telling him to put Uriah in the heat of battle?

3. Who wrote to the churches concerning the Jerusalem council's decision on the issue of circumcision?

4. Who, using John as a scribe, wrote to the seven churches in Asia?

14. 2 Maccabees (Apocrypha)
15. 2 Esdras (Apocrypha)
16. Ascension of Isaiah (Pseudipigrapha)
17. Psalms of Solomon (Pseudipigrapha)
18. Sybilline Oracles (Pseudipigrapha)
19. Book of Enoch (Pseudipigrapha)
20. Testament of the Twelve Patriarchs (Pseudipigrapha)
21. Book of Jubilees (Pseudipigrapha)
22. Targums
23. The Talmud

◆Take a Letter (Answers)

1. The Letter to the Laodiceans (Colossians 4:16)
2. Joab (2 Samuel 11:4, 15)
3. James (Acts 15:23)
4. Jesus (Revelation 1-3)

5. Who had enemies that wrote smear letters about him to the Persian king?

6. What mighty king wrote a letter to Hezekiah concerning surrender?

7. Who wrote to the people of Samaria regarding the fate of Ahab's seventy sons?

8. Who wrote a letter recommending Apollos to the Corinthians church?

9. Who wrote a letter to Felix concerning the apostle Paul?

10. Who wrote a letter granting permission to continue construction on the second temple?

11. What king received a letter from Elijah predicting judgment on his sinful reign?

12. What queen wrote to the leaders of Jezreel concerning Naboth?

13. Who asked the high priest for letters of introduction to the synagogues in Damascus?

14. Who sent letters of invitation to the tribes of Ephraim and Manasseh, asking them to join in a Passover celebration?

15. Who sent a letter giving Judah's enemies permission to stop the Jews' work on the temple?

16. What feast did Mordecai prescribe in his letters to the Jews in Persia?

17. What leper carried a letter from the king of Syria to the king of Israel?

18. Who sent a threatening letter designed to discourage Nehemiah from his plans to rebuild Jerusalem?

19. Who, with Paul, penned the First Letter to the Corinthians?

20. Who wrote to Philemon concerning his runaway slave, Onesimus?

5. Zerubbabel (Ezra 4:6-16)
 6. Sennacherib (2 Kings 19:14)
 7. Jehu (2 Kings 10:1-2)
 8. The Ephesian church (Acts 18:27)
 9. Claudius Lysias (Acts 23:25)
10. King Darius (Ezra 6:6-12)
11. Jehoram (2 Chronicles 21:12)
12. Jezebel (1 Kings 21:8)
13. Paul (Acts 9:2)
14. Hezekiah (2 Chronicles 30:1-3)
15. King Artaxerxes (Ezra 4:17-22)
16. Purim (Esther 9:20-21)
17. Naaman (2 Kings 5:5-6)
18. Sanballat (Nehemiah 6:5-7)
19. Sosthenes (1 Corinthians 1:1)
20. Paul (Philemon)

PART 7

...And Things Left Over

✦Curious Quotations

For each of the strange quotations listed, name the book of
the Bible where it is found. (If you're really good, name
the chapter and verse.)

1. At Parbar westward, four at the causeway, and two at
   Parbar.
2. Therefore will I discover thy skirts upon thy face.
3. The mountains skipped like rams, and the little hills
   like lambs.
4. All faces shall gather blackness.
5. The ships of Tarshish did sing of thee in thy market.
6. The herds of cattle are perplexed.
7. The voice of the turtle is heard in our land.
8. And they made two ouches of gold.
9. A bell and a pomegranate, a bell and a pomegranate,
   round about the hem of the robe to minister in.
10. I have put off my coat; how shall I put it on?
11. Dead flies cause the ointment of the apothecary to
    send forth a stinking savor.
12. Every man shall kiss his lips that giveth a right
    answer.
13. And kings shall be thy nursing fathers.
14. This thy stature is like to a palm tree, and thy breasts
    to clusters of grapes.
15. Destruction and death say, We have heard the fame
    thereof with our ears.
16. Associate yourselves, O ye people, and ye shall be
    broken in pieces.
17. And the rest of the trees of his forest shall be few, that
    a child may write them.

✦Curious Quotations (Answers)

1. 1 Chronicles (26:18)
2. Jeremiah (13:26)
3. Psalms (114:4)
4. Joel (2:6)
5. Ezekiel (27:25)
6. Joel (1:18)
7. Song of Solomon (2:12)
8. Exodus (39:16)
9. Exodus (39:26)
10. Song of Solomon (5:3)
11. Ecclesiastes (10:1)
12. Proverbs (24:26)
13. Isaiah (49:23)
14. Song of Solomon (7:7)
15. Job (28:22)
16. Isaiah (8:9)
17. Isaiah (10:19)

18. And on the eighth day she shall take unto her two turtles.
19. Thou shalt not seethe a kid in his mother's milk.
20. Thy lips, O my spouse, drop as the honeycomb; honey and milk are under thy tongue; and the smell of thy garments is like the smell of Lebanon.
21. And it came to pass in the first month in the second year, on the first day of the month, that the tabernacle was reared up.
22. Behold, he formed grasshoppers in the beginning of the shooting up.
23. So two or three cities wandered unto one city to drink water.
24. Let the floods clap their hands; let the hills be joyful together.
25. Every head was made bald, and every shoulder was peeled.
26. Her king is cut off as the foam upon the water.
27. And the sea coast shall be dwellings and cottages for shepherds, and folds for flocks.
28. And it waxed great, even to the host of heaven.
29. Then the king's countenance was changed, and his thoughts troubled him, so that the joints of his loins were loosed, and his knees smote one against the other.
30. He maketh them to skip like a calf; Lebanon and Sirion like a young unicorn.
31. And the wild asses did stand in the high places, they snuffed up the wind like dragons.
32. I have compared thee, O my love, to a company of horses in Pharaoh's chariots.
33. Thy bow was made quite naked.
34. The Lord will smite thee with the botch of Egypt, and with the emerods, and with the scab, and with the itch.
35. Cease ye from man, whose breath is in his nostrils.
36. Behold, I will corrupt your seed, and spread dung upon your faces, even the dung of your solemn feasts.

18. Leviticus (15:29)
19. Deuteronomy (14:21)
20. Song of Solomon (4:11)
21. Exodus (40:17)
22. Amos (7:1)
23. Amos (4:8)
24. Psalms (98:8)
25. Ezekiel (29:18)
26. Hosea (10:7)
27. Zephaniah (2:6)
28. Daniel (8:10)
29. Daniel (5:6)
30. Psalms (29:6)
31. Jeremiah (14:6)
32. Song of Solomon (1:9)
33. Habakkuk (3:9)
34. Deuteronomy (28:27)
35. Isaiah (2:22)
36. Malachi (2:3)

37. They are all adulterers, as an oven heated by the baker.

38. Feed thy people with thy rod.

39. And the man whose hair is fallen off his head, he is bald; yet is he clean.

40. Ye shall not eat one day, nor two days, nor five days, neither ten days, nor twenty days, but even a whole month, until it come out at your nostrils.

41. I am gone like the shadow when it declineth; I am tossed up and down as the locust.

42. And the unicorns shall come down with them, and the bullocks with the bulls; and their land shall be soaked with blood, and their dust made fat with fatness.

43. Thy teeth are like a flock of sheep that are even shorn, which came up from the washing.

44. The words of a man's mouth are as deep waters.

45. Lift up your heads, O ye gates.

46. Thou shalt suck the breast of kings.

47. Will I eat the flesh of bulls, or drink the blood of goats?

48. When she saw Isaac, she lighted off the camel.

49. Thy neck is like the tower of David builded for an armory, whereon there hang a thousand bucklers.

50. Thou shalt not respect persons, neither take a gift.

51. So and more also do God unto the enemies of David, if I leave of all that pertain to him by the morning light any that pisseth against the wall.

52. Moab is my washpot; over Edom will I cast out my shoe.

53. The watchman said, The morning cometh, and also the night; if ye will inquire, inquire ye; return, come.

54. And he will take your menservants, and your maidservants, and your goodliest young men, and your asses, and put them to his work.

55. Their feet are swift to shed blood.

56. Now therefore go, and I will be with thy mouth.

37. Hosea (7:4)
38. Micah (7:14)
39. Leviticus (13:40)
40. Numbers (11:19-20)
41. Psalms (109:23)
42. Isaiah (34:7)
43. Song of Solomon (4:2)
44. Proverbs (18:4)
45. Psalms (24:7)
46. Isaiah (60:16)
47. Psalms (50:13)
48. Genesis (24:64)
49. Song of Solomon (4:4)
50. Deuteronomy (16:19)
51. 1 Samuel (25:22)
52. Psalms (60:8)
53. Isaiah (21:12)
54. 1 Samuel (8:16)
55. Romans (3:15)
56. Exodus (4:12)

✦Not to Be Taken Seriously (I)

1. What New Testament book has an insect in the title?
2. Which book in the Old Testament is a math book?
3. What is the moral of the story of Jonah and the great fish?
4. What do we find in Matthew and Mark that we don't find in Luke and John?
5. Where is the first example of math in the Bible?
6. Where is the second?
7. What was the difference between the ten thousand soldiers of Israel and the three hundred Gideon chose for battle?
8. Is the Book of Josiah in the Old or New Testament?
9. What book mentions a righteous baseball pitcher?

✦Scripture on Scripture

1. According to Paul, who takes away the "veil" over the Old Testament?
2. What group of Christians examined the Scriptures every day to see if Paul was telling the truth?
3. To what young pastor did Paul address his famous words on the divine inspiration of all Scripture?
4. What apostle claimed that the prophets, in writing of the coming Christ, were writing for later generations?
5. Who told the Jews that the Scriptures had testified about him?
6. Where was Jesus when he taught two people how the prophets had predicted his death?
7. To what church did Paul say the Old Testament was written as a set of examples and warnings for the church?
8. In the parable of Lazarus and the rich man, what does Abraham say to the rich man who wants to keep his relatives out of hell?

✦Not to Be Taken Seriously (I) (Answers)

1. Ti(moth)y
2. Numbers
3. You can't keep a good man down
4. The letter *a*
5. God divided the light from the darkness
6. God told Adam to go forth and multiply
7. 9,700
8. Neither—there is no such book
9. Psalm 26:1—"Judge me, O Lord; for I have walked in mine integrity."

✦Scripture on Scripture (Answers)

1. Christ (2 Corinthians 3:14)
2. The Christians at Berea (Acts 17:11)
3. Timothy (2 Timothy 3:15-17)
4. Peter (1 Peter 1:10-12)
5. Jesus (John 5:39-40)
6. The road to Emmaus (Luke 24:25-27)
7. Corinth (1 Corinthians 10:11)
8. He tells him that the people have Moses and the prophets (Luke 16:27-29)

9. To whom does the writer of Hebrews attribute Psalm 95?
10. What apostle claimed that no Scripture had come about through the prophet's own efforts, but by God's will?
11. In what epistle does Paul promote the public reading of Scripture?
12. What foreign official did Philip teach the predictions of Jesus contained in the Old Testament?
13. In what Gospel does Jesus say that the Scripture cannot be broken?
14. To whom did Peter and John attribute the words of David (Psalm 2)?
15. To whom did Jesus say "Ye do err, not knowing the Scriptures" after they had posed a ridiculous riddle to him?

◆Differences of Opinion

Many readers are puzzled by what seem to be discrepancies in the biblical narratives. Most of these differences can be easily explained by a close reading of the text. Others may be due to errors that occur in centuries of copying manuscripts. None reflect on the inspiration of the Scriptures. I include these questions here, not to cast doubt on the Bible, but merely to test the reader's knowledge of some of these so-called discrepancies.

1. According to Genesis 25:1, Abraham's second wife was Keturah. According to 1 Chronicles 1:32, what was Keturah?
2. In Genesis 29:27, Rachel is given to Jacob seven or eight days after his marriage to Leah. According to Genesis 30:25-32, how long did Jacob have to wait for Rachel?

9. The Holy Spirit (Hebrews 3:7)
10. Peter (2 Peter 1:20)
11. 1 Timothy (4:13)
12. The Ethiopian eunuch (Acts 8:32-35)
13. John (10:35)
14. The Holy Spirit (Acts 4:25)
15. The Sadducees (Matthew 22:29)

◆Differences of Opinion (Answers)

1. His concubine
2. Fourteen years

3. In Exodus 33:20, God tells Moses that no man can see God's face. According to Exodus 33:11, what man saw God face to face?

4. The Levites entered the service of the sanctuary at age thirty—according to Numbers 4:3. At what age, according to Numbers 8:24, did they enter the service?

5. The mission of the twelve Israelite spies started from Paran—according to Numbers 13:3. In Numbers 20:1, where does the mission start?

6. According to Deuteronomy 10:6, Aaron died at Moserah. Where, according to Numbers 20:28, did he die?

7. Deuteronomy 15:4 says "There shall be no poor among you." What does Deuteronomy 15:11 say?

8. According to 1 Samuel 16:10-11, David had eight brothers. How many in 1 Chronicles 2:13-15 did he have?

9. In 1 Samuel 16:19-21, David comes to know Saul by being employed as his harpist. In 1 Samuel 17, how does David come to know Saul?

10. In 1 Samuel 17, David is the slayer of Goliath. According to 2 Samuel 21:19, who killed the giant?

11. In 1 Samuel 31:3-4, Saul takes his own life after being wounded. In 2 Samuel 1, who claims he actually killed Saul?

12. Absalom had, according to 2 Samuel 14:27, three sons. How many did he have, according to 2 Samuel 18:18?

13. The Lord moved David to number the people of Israel, according to 2 Samuel 24:1. Who, in the story in 1 Chronicles 21, moved David to do this?

14. According to 2 Kings 24:8, King Jehoiachin was eighteen years old when he began to reign. How old was he in the account in 2 Chronicles 36?

15. Samuel was an Ephraimite, according to 1 Samuel 1. What tribe was he from in the account in 1 Chronicles 6?

3. Moses
4. Twenty-five
5. Kadesh
6. Mount Hor
7. "The poor will never cease to be in the land."
8. Seven
9. Through the killing of Goliath
10. Elhanan
11. Saul's Amalekite bodyguard
12. None
13. Satan
14. Eight
15. Levi

16. According to 2 Chronicles 33:13-16, evil King Manasseh repented of his sins after being held captive in Babylon. What does the parallel account in 2 Kings 21 say about this repentance?

17. In Matthew's genealogy of the Messiah, Jesus is descended from David's son Solomon. What son of David is, in Luke's account, Jesus' ancestor?

18. In Luke's account of the temptation of Jesus, the last temptation is to jump from the pinnacle of the temple. What is the last temptation in Matthew's version?

19. According to Matthew 8:5-13, a centurion asks that his servant be healed. In Luke 7:2-11, who does the asking?

20. In Matthew 8, the maniac lives in Gadara. In Luke 8 and Mark 5, where does he live?

21. Matthew 20:20 states that the mother of James and John requested that her sons be appointed to high office in the coming kingdom. In Mark 10:35, who made the request?

22. In Matthew 26:34, Jesus predicts that Peter will betray him before the rooster crows once. In Mark 14:30, how many times is the rooster supposed to crow?

23. According to Matthew 27:3-10, Judas hanged himself. How, according to Acts 1:18, did he kill himself?

24. In John 19:19, we are told that the inscription of the cross read, "Jesus of Nazareth, the King of the Jews." According to Matthew 27:37, what was the inscription?

25. In Mark 2:26, Jesus says that Abiathar was priest during David's reign. Who, according to 1 Samuel 21, was priest at that time?

26. Matthew 5:3 has Jesus saying, "Blessed are the poor in spirit." What does he say in Luke 6:20?

16. Nothing
17. Nathan
18. The temptation to rule the world
19. The servant
20. Gerasa
21. James and John
22. Twice
23. He fell headlong and burst apart
24. "This is Jesus, the King of the Jews."
25. Abimelech
26. "Blessed are the poor."

27. James 1:13 says God does not tempt men. But Genesis 22:1 says God tempted a certain man. Who?

28. Solomon had 40,000 horses, according to 1 Kings 4:26. How many did he have according to 2 Chronicles 9:25?

29. Matthew 27:6-8 says the priests bought the potter's field, but Acts 1:18-19 says someone else bought it. Who?

30. Matthew 27:9-10 attributes the prophecy about the potter's field to Jeremiah. Where is the prophecy found?

31. Mark 15:26 says the inscription on Jesus' cross read "The King of the Jews." What is it in Luke's account (23:38)?

32. Matthew's genealogy of Jesus says that Joseph's father was Jacob (1:16). According to Luke 3:23, who was it?

33. In what epistle does Paul say "Bear ye one another's burdens" and "Every man shall bear his own burden."

34. What book says, in the same chapter, "Answer not a fool according to his folly" and "Answer a fool according to his folly."

35. David's wife Michal had, according to 2 Samuel 6:23, no children. But according to 2 Samuel 21:8 she had children. How many?

36. Solomon stated in Proverbs 18:22, "Whoso findeth a wife findeth a good thing." Who, in the New Testament, stated, "It is good for a man not to touch a woman"?

37. Acts 9:7 says that the people traveling with Paul heard the heavenly voice Paul heard. But, according to Acts 22:9, someone said that the people did not hear the voice. Who said that?

27. Abraham
28. 4,000
29. Judas Iscariot
30. Zechariah 11:12,13. Neither Jeremiah nor Zechariah quotes the prophecy as it is quoted in Matthew.
31. "This Is the King of the Jews."
32. Heli
33. Galatians (6:2 and 6:5)
34. Proverbs (26:4 and 26:5)
35. Five. (This apparent scribal error is corrected in some translations, where Merab, not Michal, is the mother of the five children.)
36. Paul (1 Corinthians 7)
37. Paul

38. Mark 1:12-13 says that Jesus immediately went into the wilderness after his baptism and was there for forty days. Which Gospel claims that the day after his baptism he called Andrew and Peter to be his disciples?

39. According to 1 Corinthians 15:5, Jesus appeared to the twelve disciples after his resurrection. According to Matthew and Acts, how many apostles were there after his resurrection?

◆They Did It First

In the Bible . . .

1. What is the first dream mentioned?
2. What is the first war mentioned?
3. Where was the first piggy bank?
4. What is the first commandment?
5. What is the first purchase of land?
6. What was the first instance of book burning?
7. What was the first military coup in Israel?
8. Where did Jesus work his first miracle?
9. What was the first of the ten plagues of Egypt?
10. Who told the first lie?
11. What was the first city called?
12. What was the first animal out of the ark?
13. Where were the disciples first called Christians?
14. Who planted the first garden?
15. What is the first commandment with a promise attached to it?
16. What is the first color mentioned?

38. John (1:35)
39. Only eleven. Matthew 27:3-5 says that Judas Iscariot hanged himself before Jesus' resurrection, and Acts 1:9-26 says that the new apostle, Matthias, had not yet been chosen at the time of the Resurrection.

◆They Did It First (Answers)

1. The dream of Abimelech, in which he was told to return Sarah to Abraham (Genesis 20:3-8)
2. The war of the kings of the north, led by Chedorlaomer, king of Elam (Genesis 14)
3. In the temple at Jerusalem. It was a chest, ordered by King Joash, who had a hole bored in the lid to keep priests from stealing funds (2 Kings 12).
4. "Be fruitful and multiply" (Genesis 1:28)
5. Abraham bought the Cave of Machpelah as a tomb for Sarah (Genesis 23:3-20)
6. Jeremiah's scroll, sent to King Jehoiakim, was burnt piece by piece as it was being read to the king (Jeremiah 36:21-23)
7. Absalom led an attempt to overthrow his father, David (2 Samuel 15–18)
8. Cana (John 2:1-11)
9. The river turned to blood (Exodus 7:14-24)
10. The serpent (Genesis 3:4)
11. Enoch, named after Cain's son (Genesis 4:17)
12. The raven (Genesis 8:7)
13. Antioch (Acts 11:26)
14. God (Genesis 2:8)
15. "Honor your father and mother" (Deuteronomy 5:16, Ephesians 6:2-3). The promise is that the person will have a long life if he honors his parents.
16. Green—"I have given every green herb" (Genesis 1:30)

❖A Few Bits of Potpourri

1. Which Gospel was, according to tradition, written first?
2. Which epistle was called "an epistle of straw" by Martin Luther, who disliked it because he thought it taught salvation by works?
3. What New Testament book had the most difficulty being accepted as Scripture by the early Christians?
4. What Egyptian bishop was the first person to list the 27 New Testament books that we now have?
5. What American president published an edition of the Gospels which left out all the supernatural elements?
6. Who printed the first Bible?
7. What year did that occur?
8. What conqueror said, "The Bible is no mere book, but a Living Creature, with a power that conquers all that oppose it"?
9. What world-famous author said, "The New Testament is the very best book that ever was or ever will be known in the world"?
10. What was the name of the Jewish scholars who first inserted vowels into the text of the Hebrew Old Testament?
11. What year was the first American Bible printed?
12. Who was the first person to use the term *New Testament* to refer to the Christian Scriptures?
13. What three languages was the Bible originally written in?
14. What form of Greek was the New Testament written in?
15. What material were the first manuscripts of the New Testament written on?
16. What president, speaking of the Bible, said, "That book is the rock on which our republic rests"?
17. What language was the first American Bible in?

◆A Few Bits of Potpourri (Answers)

1. Mark
2. James
3. Revelation
4. Athanasius of Alexandria. This occurred in A.D. 367.
5. Thomas Jefferson
6. Johann Gutenberg
7. 1456
8. Napoleon
9. Charles Dickens
10. The Masoretes
11. 1752, in Boston
12. Tertullian of Carthage, around A.D. 200. Writing in Latin, Tertullian actually called the Scriptures *Novum Testamentum.*
13. Hebrew and Aramaic (Old Testament) and Greek (New Testament)
14. Koine, the common Greek of the Roman Empire
15. Papyrus, a material made from strips of reeds
16. Andrew Jackson
17. Algonquin Indian. The translation was done in 1663 by John Eliot, a missionary to the Indians. Not until the Revolutionary War was the English Bible printed in America. Prior to the War, all English Bibles were brought over from England.

◆Not to Be Taken Seriously (II)

1. What is the first medicine mentioned in the Bible?
2. What book of the New Testament contains a fruit in its title?
3. How many books in the Old Testament were named after Esther?
4. How do we know God has a sense of humor?
5. During the days of creation, what weighed less—the days or the nights?
6. Where were freeways first mentioned in the Bible?
7. Where does the Bible talk about the power of TV and radio?
8. Why did the tower of Babel stand in the land of Shinar?
9. Where is baseball first mentioned in the Bible?
10. Where is the second mention?
11. And the third?

✦Not to Be Taken Seriously (II) (Answers)

1. The two tablets God gave to Moses
2. Phi(lemon)
3. Twenty-two—the rest were named before Esther
4. He can take a rib
5. The days—they were light
6. Genesis 1:30—"The Lord made every creeping thing"
7. Esther 1:3—"The power of Persia and Media"
8. It would have looked funny lying on its side
9. Genesis 3:6—Eve stole first, Adam stole second
10. Judges 7:20—Gideon and his men rattled their pitchers
11. Psalm 26:1—"I shall not slide"

Other Living Books® Best-Sellers

THE ANGEL OF HIS PRESENCE by Grace Livingston Hill. This book captures the romance of John Wentworth Stanley and a beautiful young woman whose influence causes John to re-evaluate his well-laid plans for the future. 07-0047-3 $3.95.

ANSWERS by Josh McDowell and Don Stewart. In a question-and-answer format, the authors tackle sixty-five of the most-asked questions about the Bible, God, Jesus Christ, miracles, other religions, and creation. 07-0021-X $4.95.

THE BEST CHRISTMAS PAGEANT EVER by Barbara Robinson. A delightfully wild and funny story about what happens to a Christmas program when the "Horrible Herdman" brothers and sisters are miscast in the roles of the biblical Christmas story characters. 07-0137-2 $3.95.

BUILDING YOUR SELF-IMAGE by Josh McDowell. Here are practical answers to help you overcome your fears, anxieties, and lack of self-confidence. Learn how God's higher image of who you are can take root in your heart and mind. 07-1395-8 $4.95.

THE CHILD WITHIN by Mari Hanes. The author shares insights she gained from God's Word during her own pregnancy. She identifies areas of stress, offers concrete data about the birth process, and points to God's sure promises that he will "gently lead those that are with young." 07-0219-0 $3.95.

COME BEFORE WINTER AND SHARE MY HOPE by Charles R. Swindoll. A collection of brief vignettes offering hope and the assurance that adversity and despair are temporary setbacks we can overcome! 07-0477-0 $6.95.

DARE TO DISCIPLINE by James Dobson. A straightforward, plainly written discussion about building and maintaining parent/child relationships based upon love, respect, authority, and ultimate loyalty to God. 07-0522-X $4.95.

DR. DOBSON ANSWERS YOUR QUESTIONS by James Dobson. In this convenient reference book, renowned author Dr. James Dobson addresses heartfelt concerns on many topics including questions on marital relationships, infant care, child discipline, home management, and others. 07-0580-7 $5.95.

Other Living Books® Best-Sellers

FOR MEN ONLY edited by J. Allan Petersen. This book deals with topics of concern to every man: the business world, marriage, fathering, spiritual goals, and problems of living as a Christian in a secular world. 07-0892-X $4.95.

FOR WOMEN ONLY by Evelyn and J. Allan Petersen. Balanced, entertaining, diversified treatment of all aspects of womanhood. 07-0897-0 $5.95.

400 WAYS TO SAY I LOVE YOU by Alice Chapin. Perhaps the flame of love has almost died in your marriage. Maybe you have a good marriage that just needs a little "spark." Here is a book especially for the woman who wants to rekindle the flame of romance in her marriage, who wants creative, practical, useful ideas to show the man in her life that she cares. 07-0919-5 $3.95.

GIVERS, TAKERS, AND OTHER KINDS OF LOVERS by Josh McDowell and Paul Lewis. This book bypasses vague generalities about love and sex and gets right to the basic questions: Whatever happened to sexual freedom? What's true love like? Do men respond differently than women? If you're looking for straight answers about God's plan for love and sexuality, this book was written for you. 07-1031-2 $3.95.

HINDS' FEET ON HIGH PLACES by Hannah Hurnard. A classic allegory of a journey toward faith that has sold more than a million copies! 07-1429-6 $4.95.

HOW TO BE HAPPY THOUGH MARRIED by Tim LaHaye. One of America's most successful marriage counselors gives practical, proven advice for marital happiness. 07-1499-7 $3.95.

THE INTIMATE MARRIAGE by R. C. Sproul. The author focuses on biblical patterns of marriage and practical ways to develop intimacy. Discussion questions included at end of each chapter. 07-1610-8 $3.95.

JOHN, SON OF THUNDER by Ellen Gunderson Traylor. In this saga of adventure, romance, and discovery, travel with John—the disciple whom Jesus loved—down desert paths, through the courts of the Holy City, to the foot of the cross, as he leaves his luxury as a privileged son of Israel for the bitter hardship of his exile on Patmos. 07-1903-4 $5.95

Other Living Books® Best-Sellers

LIFE IS TREMENDOUS! by Charlie "Tremendous" Jones. Believing that enthusiasm makes the difference, Jones shows how anyone can be happy, involved, relevant, productive, healthy, and secure in the midst of a high-pressure, commercialized society. 07-2184-5 $3.95.

LORD, COULD YOU HURRY A LITTLE? by Ruth Harms Calkin. These prayer-poems from the heart of a godly woman trace the inner workings of the heart, following the rhythms of the day and seasons of the year with expectation and love. 07-3816-0 $3.95.

LORD, I KEEP RUNNING BACK TO YOU by Ruth Harms Calkin. In prayer-poems tinged with wonder, joy, humanness, and questioning, the author speaks for all of us who are groping and learning together what it means to be God's child. 07-3819-5 $3.95.

MORE THAN A CARPENTER by Josh McDowell. A hard-hitting book for people who are skeptical about Jesus' deity, his resurrection, and his claim on their lives. 07-4552-3 $3.95.

MOUNTAINS OF SPICES by Hannah Hurnard. Here is an allegory comparing the nine spices mentioned in the Song of Solomon to the nine fruits of the Spirit. A story of the glory of surrender by the author of *Hinds' Feet on High Places*. 07-4611-2 $4.95.

NOW IS YOUR TIME TO WIN by Dave Dean. In this true-life story, Dean shares how he locked into seven principles that enabled him to bounce back from failure to success. Read about successful men and women—from sports and entertainment celebrities to the ordinary people next door—and discover how you too can bounce back from failure to success! 07-4727-5 $3.95.

THE SECRET OF LOVING by Josh McDowell. McDowell explores the values and qualities that will help both single and married readers to be the right person for someone else. He offers a fresh perspective for evaluating and improving the reader's love life. 07-5845-5 $4.95.

THE STORY FROM THE BOOK. The full sweep of *The Book*'s contents in abridged, chronological form, giving the reader the "big picture" of the Bible. 07-6677-6 $4.95.

Other Living Books® Best-Sellers

STRIKE THE ORIGINAL MATCH by Charles Swindoll. Many couples ask: What do you do when the warm, passionate fire that once lit your marriage begins to wane? Here, Chuck Swindoll provides biblical steps for rekindling the fires of romance and building marital intimacy. 07-6445-5 $4.95.

SUCCESS: THE GLENN BLAND METHOD by Glenn Bland. The author shows how to set goals and make plans that really work. His ingredients of success include spiritual, financial, educational, and recreational balances. 07-6689-6 $4.95.

THROUGH GATES OF SPLENDOR by Elisabeth Elliot. This unforgettable story of five men who braved the Auca Indians has become one of the most famous missionary books of all times. 07-7151-6 $4.95.

WHAT WIVES WISH THEIR HUSBANDS KNEW ABOUT WOMEN by James Dobson. The best-selling author of *Dare to Discipline* and *The Strong-Willed Child* brings us this vital book that speaks to the unique emotional needs and aspirations of today's woman. An immensely practical, interesting guide. 07-7896-0 $4.95.

WHY YOU ACT THE WAY YOU DO by Tim LaHaye. Discover how your temperament affects your work, emotions, spiritual life, and relationships, and learn how to make improvements. 07-8212-7 $4.95.